A FAIR WORLD FOR ALL

Dedicated to
>the people of my home town,
>>Arlington, Vermont, U.S.A.,
because since the foundation of the town in 1764, they have, like many another peaceable, hard-working community all around the globe, proved in the factual field of everyday life the truth of the idea on which the United Nations is based—that men and women, each one full to the brim of human nature, can, by the act of living together, create for all more safety, more opportunity, and more hope.

[An interpretation based on a study of official records of the debates concerning the Universal Declaration of Human Rights, and on consultations with members of the United Nations Department of Social Affairs, the Department of Public Information, and the Educational, Scientific and Cultural Organization.]

WHITTLESEY HOUSE

McGRAW-HILL BOOK COMPANY, INC.

New York   London   Toronto

A FAIR WORLD FOR ALL

THE MEANING OF THE
DECLARATION OF HUMAN RIGHTS

by DOROTHY
CANFIELD
FISHER

with a foreword by ELEANOR ROOSEVELT

illustrated by JEANNE BENDICK

Library of Congress Catalog Card Number: 52-9451

Published by Whittlesey House
A division of the McGraw-Hill Book Company, Inc.

PRINTED IN THE UNITED STATES OF AMERICA

Foreword

Tʜɪs ʟɪᴛᴛʟᴇ ʙᴏᴏᴋ ꜰᴏʀ ʏᴏᴜɴɢ ᴘᴇᴏᴘʟᴇ, ᴏʀ ɪɴ-
deed for people of any age, has been written by
Dorothy Canfield Fisher to explain in everyday language the Universal Declaration of Human Rights.

This Declaration is a landmark in civilization and
was written not by any one country or group of
countries, but by the 58 nations that were part of
the United Nations, and for many nations that had
not yet joined the United Nations.

On the basis of her broad experience and deep
understanding, Mrs. Fisher has brought her own
interpretation to the text of the Universal Declaration. During the writing of this book, Mrs. Fisher
studied all the official records of the United Nations debates on the Declaration, and concerning
them she sought the advice of officials in the Department of Social Affairs, the Department of Public Information, and UNESCO.

As a member of the Commission on Human
Rights from the beginning, I can say that the Declaration was drafted in conformity with the pro-
visions of the Charter of the United Nations under
which members of the United Nations agreed to
promote human rights and fundamental freedoms.

It was approved by the General Assembly of the United Nations as a declaration of standards and aspirations for all peoples everywhere.

At first it was hoped that this Declaration could be made short enough to be memorized by everybody, but as the work progressed, it was found difficult to omit any of the thoughts finally included.

The rights of human beings, as well as the responsibilities that go with them, are indeed very numerous and very great. Some persons felt that the responsibilities should have been stressed with every right. We felt that we had to stress the rights and that one article stating the fact that responsibilities did go with every right would be sufficient.

It is good for young people to have this responsibility in terms that they can understand, since here are standards which they must consider in their relationship with the peoples of the world.

Eleanor Roosevelt

THE UNITED STATES REPRESENTATIVE ON THE
UNITED NATIONS HUMAN RIGHTS COMMISSION

PREAMBLE—

WHEREAS recognition of the inherent dignity and of the equal and inalienable rights of all members of the human family is the foundation of freedom, justice and peace in the world,

WHEREAS disregard and contempt for human rights have resulted in barbarous acts which have outraged the conscience of mankind, and the advent of a world in which human beings shall enjoy freedom of speech and belief and freedom from fear and want has been proclaimed as the highest aspiration of the common people,

WHEREAS it is essential, if man is not to be compelled to have recourse, as a last resort, to rebellion against tyranny and oppression, that human rights should be protected by the rule of law,

WHEREAS it is essential to promote the development of friendly relations between nations,

WHEREAS the peoples of the United Nations have in the Charter reaffirmed their faith in fundamental human rights, in the dignity and worth of the human person and in the equal rights of men and women and have determined to promote social progress and better standards of life in larger freedom,

WHEREAS Member States have pledged themselves to achieve, in cooperation with the United Nations, the promotion of universal respect for and observance of human rights and fundamental freedoms,

WHEREAS a common understanding of these rights and freedoms is of the greatest importance for the full realization of this pledge,

7

Now Therefore

THE GENERAL ASSEMBLY PROCLAIMS

This Univeral Declaration of Human Rights as a common standard of achievement for all peoples and all nations, to the end that every individual and every organ of society, keeping this Declaration constantly in mind, shall strive by teaching and education to promote respect for these rights and freedoms and by progressive measures, national and international, to secure their universal and effective recognition and observance, both among the peoples of Member States themselves and among the peoples of territories under their jurisdiction.

Ideas We All Agree On

A GOOD MANY YEARS AGO, IN 1893, A BIG World's Fair was held in a big city. In its buildings samples were shown of the tools used by men and women all over the world in their daily work. The hope was that visitors to the Fair might get some hints about how to improve their own ways of living and working.

There were so many buildings that the place looked like a city. Inside them thousands of useful inventions and devices were shown. Take plows, for instance. There was a little wooden plow made of a crooked stick, to be drawn by a camel or maybe a donkey. Next to this perhaps was a great shining steel plow to be drawn by twenty horses or a steam-driven tractor. They were so different they really looked funny, standing side by side.

9

Yet the crowds of visitors didn't need anybody to tell them that both these plows, and all the other plows in the Fair, had the very same purpose—to break up the ground so that seed could be planted to grow more food for human families.

Pumps were shown—all kinds of pumps. Some were run by a big wheel to be pushed around by a horse. Some ran by electricity, so that all they needed was somebody to push a button and to oil the moving parts once in a while. Yet every pump had the same purpose—to get water where men and women needed water.

The buildings at the World's Fair were very different from each other, too. Some were small, with thatched roofs. Others were many stories tall and had elevators.

But back of every one of them was the same idea—to make a place protected from bad weather for men, women, and children to live in, where they could keep their belongings and their tools, and have a fire for cooking.

There is more to human life than eating and drinking, getting clothes to wear, and having a place to live where rain and snow can't come in. The life of the human spirit is ever so much more important. In this meeting of people from many lands the inner life had a place, too. These men and women from all around the globe had a chance to compare their ideas about right and wrong, and the best way to live.

A Congress of Religions was held in a great hall set in the midst of the plows, the looms for weaving, the lathes, the saws. People came to it from everywhere. There were representatives of Buddhism, Christianity, Mohammedanism, Zoroastrism, Shintoism. Never before had people of so many different religions come together.

No two of them looked alike: some wore long, bright-colored robes, some were dressed in black broadcloth suits; some wore turbans on their heads, some close-fitting small caps; some had great beards and long hair, some shaved their faces closely and some even shaved their heads. Most of them had never laid eyes on each other before. Some of them had never before even seen anybody with a religion unlike theirs.

But when they began to talk to each other, they found that, among the purposes of their differing religions, one purpose was the same in all—to teach men and women how to manage their lives so that they would do not harm but good to their fellow men.

Each faith was unlike the others in the answers it gave to such tremendous questions as:

What is our human place in the universe?

What is the real inner meaning of our human lives?

Do we go on living after death?

How should we pray, and what should we pray for?

Above all—*Why* should we try to do good and not evil?

When the talk was about such deep mysteries, the reverend representatives of the world's churches, mosques, meetinghouses, synagogues, and temples could hardly understand each other's words. But when they were comparing notes about their ideas of the way human beings should treat each other in daily life, every single religious leader in turn said that his religion tried to make its believers kind, honest, generous, willing to give other people a fair chance.

That was long ago. Since then men and women of the world have been coming together. Rapid steamships, trains, airplanes, radio, telephones, fast mail service—all have brought us so close together that, whether we wish it or not, we are neighbors. The whole world is now our neighborhood. We must learn to be good neighbors. All but a few of the countries on our globe have now joined in a group called the United Nations. Their hope is that, putting their heads together, and keeping in touch with each other, they can learn to make human life more like what we all want; and especially they hope to find out how nations can live without fighting wars.

Like the representatives of the world religions in 1893, the representatives of the United Nations do not look alike. Some are men and some are women. Some wear silk robes and soft slippers; others wear tweeds and heavy-soled leather shoes. Even if they all dressed alike, they wouldn't look the same, because some are short and slightly built, others are big and brawny; some have dark skins, others are fairer. And the ways of living in their various countries are just as different as their looks.

When the delegates to the United Nations first met and began to get acquainted with each other, their ways of living seemed so far apart they hardly saw how they could ever agree on anything. But

very soon, like the representatives from the religions of the world, these representatives from the governments of the world saw that many of their ideas about human life were the same. They felt that the countries which hoped for the same things could work together better if they knew just what those hopes were.

It was the representative from the small country of Panama who got into words the idea they were all trying to express and to act on. He said: "The rights of the individual do not spring from the fact that he is a citizen of a given state, but from the fact that, like every man and woman, he is a member of the human family."

Yes, when you think of it, you can see that he spoke the truth. Suppose, going along to do an errand, you see a man standing under a big tree. He's a stranger to you, you never saw him before, maybe; you don't take any special interest in him. But if, as you walk past him, you see that the big tree begins to fall over without his no-

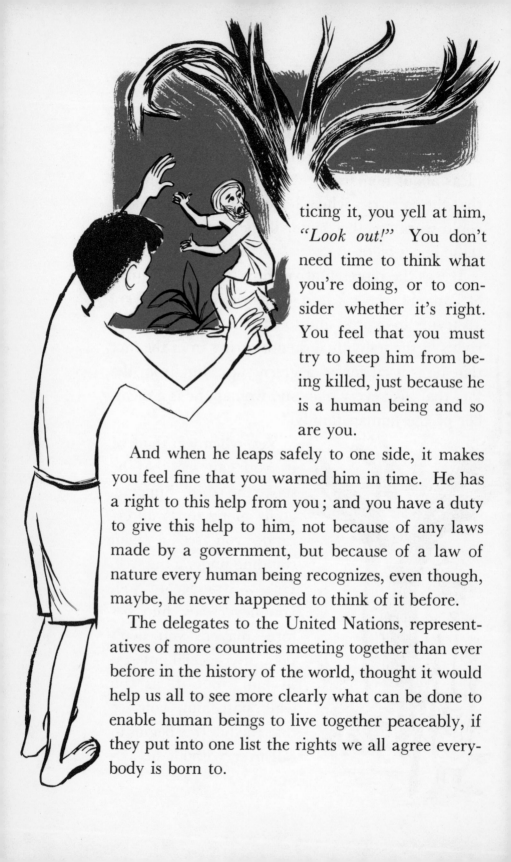

ticing it, you yell at him, *"Look out!"* You don't need time to think what you're doing, or to consider whether it's right. You feel that you must try to keep him from being killed, just because he is a human being and so are you.

And when he leaps safely to one side, it makes you feel fine that you warned him in time. He has a right to this help from you; and you have a duty to give this help to him, not because of any laws made by a government, but because of a law of nature every human being recognizes, even though, maybe, he never happened to think of it before.

The delegates to the United Nations, representatives of more countries meeting together than ever before in the history of the world, thought it would help us all to see more clearly what can be done to enable human beings to live together peaceably, if they put into one list the rights we all agree everybody is born to.

As to getting those rights legally enforced by our governments, that would have to be managed in varying ways, because climates, established customs, and ways of life are different.

For instance, one of the human rights is that everybody should have enough to eat to keep him from starving. More than this, everyone should have enough of the right kind of food to keep him healthy so that he can be useful to his community, and so that he can himself enjoy life.

Everybody, from the North Pole to the South Pole, would vote "Yes" on the proposition that life should be arranged so that everybody has enough to eat. That is one "basic human right" about which there wouldn't be any disagreement.

But there would be many disputes and misunderstandings, if anyone tried to lay down a law as to what food to eat. Bananas and rice are all right, but to say that every Eskimo ought to have bananas to eat would be as foolish as to say that in Italy or Central Africa there should be enough seal meat to go around.

Another basic right is that everybody should have shelter from bad weather. You couldn't find anybody to say "No" to that idea. But the kind of shelter that would serve in India is very different from what people in Norway need. Such details are better left to each group of people to settle according to their situation.

Where two much-traveled highways cross each other, plans should be made to keep traffic from getting snarled up. Anybody knows that much. The "traffic" can be baby carriages being pushed to a park, or elephants pulling loads of tree trunks, or high-speed automobiles, or camels, or bicycles, or oxcarts, or people on horseback. No matter how the traveling is done, some way must be invented to prevent the travelers from going ahead, each on his own, banging into other people, piling up in confusion. That's a "basic" idea.

What's not basic is the variety of ways that could be thought up to prevent collisions. One plan might be a rule that every two minutes those coming from the north and south should stop to give those coming from the east and west a chance to cross. That would prevent accidents, all right; but of course it would slow things down. Maybe it would be better to have the north and south road built up high over the crossroads, or the east and west road run through a tunnel. But suppose somebody coming from the north wanted to make a left turn to get on the road going east? Some way would have to be invented to manage that.

We may not invent the same ways to manage a situation, but we all agree on the "basic idea" of making plans for order and safety and decency and fairness in all situations.

The representatives of the many peoples of the world, meeting together in the United Nations, thought it would be useful to make a list of such basic ideas as most human beings recognize as true. The job of drawing up such a list of rights was entrusted to a committee made up of representatives of eighteen different nations which was known as the Commission on Human Rights. Later on, years later perhaps, when humanity has had a chance to get used to the idea that although we differ in many ways we have a great many ideas in common, we can get together to see what we can do about enforcing these human rights by laws. As a matter of fact, many of them have been enforced by law, everywhere, for many centuries. In no country of the globe is one human being allowed by law to murder another or to steal what belongs to another.

The first members of the Commission on Human Rights were the representatives from Australia, Belgium, Byelorussian Soviet Socialist Republic, Chile, China, Egypt, France, India, Iran, Lebanon, Panama, Philippines, Ukrainian Soviet Socialist Republic, Union of Soviet Socialist Republics, United Kingdom, United States, Uruguay, Yugoslavia. If you try to look them up in a geography, you'll need to go all around the globe to find them.

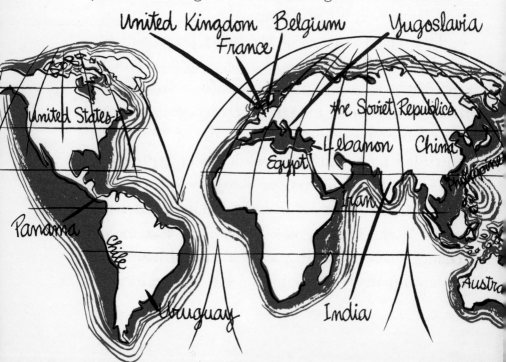

The Commission went to work seriously on the task of drawing up a Declaration of Human Rights in January 1947. A good many lists of basic human rights had already been put together by other organizations. All these were considered. There were more than fifty articles in some of them. But the United Nations Commission found they couldn't agree on so many. They wanted to be sure that they didn't put in a single idea unless everybody (or nearly everybody) felt it to be true. For nearly two years they discussed and talked over these principles, hour after hour, day after day, month after month.

By the autumn of 1948 the text of the Declaration was ready for consideration by the United Nations' highest body, the General Assembly, which was meeting that year in the Palais de Chaillot in Paris. Now don't think that all the Assembly wanted to do was to look at the Declaration hastily, tell the Commission that they had done a fine job, and adopt it. Not at all. The General Assembly represents all the nations in the United Nations— fifty-eight of them that September 1948 in Paris. All of them wanted to have a chance to discuss the Declaration. And they did just that for ten long weeks in the Third Committee in which every nation had a seat. They worked over it article by article, sentence by sentence, sometimes word by word. After the first seventeen days' discussion only the first two articles had been adopted, but they kept right at it and by the first week in December they had the Declaration ready for final approval by the plenary session of the General Assembly.

They *discussed,* you see, they didn't argufy. What's the difference? Well, when you start to argufy about something with other people, you don't want to find out what the best idea is. You want to make them accept *your* idea. You act as if you were playing a game. You are in it to win. You want to beat the other side.

Discussion isn't a bit like that. It is more like what is done when people are trying to get out of a dangerous region to a place where they will be safer and happier. When they come to a spot where the road or path isn't clear, they are terribly anxious lest they lose their way. They put their heads together to try to find out which direction is the right one. Nobody wants to force the others to accept his idea, because nobody is sure which way is exactly right. Everybody's brains and good will are needed to make the decision. Everybody's opinion is listened to and talked over. They wanted desperately to find out what the nations of the world really could agree on. And they did find out.

The day of voting was 10 December 1948. The vote was by roll call. The representative of each nation rose in turn and indicated where his nation stood on this Universal Declaration of Human Rights. When the count was in, forty-eight nations had voted in favor of the Declaration and none had voted against it. A few delegates abstained. A delegate "abstained" from voting when he wasn't quite sure he was justified in voting "Yes" but was entirely sure that he didn't want to vote "No."

That is how the Declaration of Human Rights came into being. On 10 December 1948. Remember the day, 10 December 1948.

The thirty articles, although brief, have a lot of meanings. Many of them cover abstract shades of the same idea. Yet each one is based on a single general principle. So the comments in this book have been based on the main idea in each article. Much more could be said about each of the finely drawn distinctions, written with so much care and skill by those eighteen men and women during their two years of hard work.

But we have all noticed that in our first meeting with a person or an idea, we get only a general impression. Later on, when we get better acquainted, we see the smaller details. This book tries to give such a first, general impression of the idea of each article.

We'll all come to know them better, later on, as men and women unite more closely on the many, many ideas we all agree on—even if, in a few cases, we never happened to think of them before.

ARTICLE 1

*All human beings are born free
and equal in dignity and rights.
They are endowed with reason
and conscience and should act towards one another in a spirit of
brotherhood.*

MAYBE, IN YOUR HEART, YOU HAVE THOUGHT
that there is some nonsense about the talk of all
men being brothers. Such a feeling isn't at all what
people expect of you, and so you have perhaps not
wanted to say it right out. But it is quite possible
that you have silently asked yourself, "How *can* I
feel towards a person I don't know, that 'he is a
brother'? I know that's the proper thing to say,
but I don't feel so."

Yes you do, too, if you really think about it.
Here are some ways to put it to yourself so that
you can see that you do.

Suppose that you, with a group of neighbors, are in a market or a food shop, buying bread and fish and fruit and other things to eat. Everybody is relaxed and easy, standing around waiting for his turn to buy.

All of a sudden, a big snake (maybe brought in on a bunch of fruit) crawls along a beam of the roof and drops down amongst the shoppers. You don't need anybody to tell you how most of the crowd will scream and rush for the door, while others will try to get the creature into a basket and shut the lid down, or if they can't do that, to kill it. Just as you snatch your hand away instantly from a hot piece of iron, everybody there feels that human beings must be protected from danger.

Or, here's another picture—suppose in the same food market or grocery store, as people stand around looking at prices and waiting for a chance to buy, somebody sees through the open door a big black panther (maybe escaped from a menagerie, maybe come in from the woods) racing down the street. Not a human being in the world would stop to ask those around him, "Don't you agree with me that we had better close the door?"

Not much! He'd *know* they agree with him, he'd yell and dive to slam the door shut, and the minute the others saw what he saw, they would feel just what he feels.

But suppose that you all saw a man and a woman coming towards the shop. He might be a very queer-looking man, much taller or much shorter than the men you were used to; she might have a different-colored skin from anybody you ever saw;

but from as far away as you could see them, every-body would recognize them as man and woman. Nobody would yell, nobody would slam the door shut, nobody would get out a gun. You might wonder about the man's odd clothes, you might think the color of the woman's skin was queer, but if it turned out they wanted to come in to buy food, you'd all just move over to give them room.

You take this for granted, don't you? If you think about it at all, you feel it is natural. Well, it's not. It is something which has slowly been learned. Thousands of years ago people feared a human being they didn't personally know as we now fear a wild animal.

In those human beginnings of our history, a family lived in a cave, or maybe in a small hut—father, mother, children. They knew each other, probably also a grandparent or two, and maybe some neighbors who lived in a cave nearby. But that was all. At the sight of a strange man they acted like the people in the food store when they saw a panther. The children were taught to run,

run, run back to the safety of the cave: the feeble old folks tried to hide; the strongest of the grown-ups rushed to kill the stranger, or anyhow to tie him up and to take him prisoner. They did it for the same reason—to protect themselves from danger. A stranger was as unknown to them as a panther. For all they knew he might be as dangerous.

Little by little the circle has enlarged in which men recognized other men— even strangers—as like themselves, not like unknown dangerous animals. First there were more huts close together, making a group where everybody came to know everybody else by sight. Then some of the children, as they grew up, moved to another nearby group of huts; and they were known to the first group as they came and went. At least, before people hurried to kill a strange figure, they took time for one look at him, to see if he was their kind of being.

Then, slowly, they began to notice that everybody human was the same kind of being as themselves. When fierce beasts of prey appeared, men could be pretty sure that they were going to attack to kill. Hence the safe thing to do was to attack first. But long experience taught human beings that a strange man might have in his mind some purpose entirely different from murderous attack—

maybe he had something to sell, or wanted to buy
something they had; maybe he came to warn them
of a forest fire or a flood; maybe he was lost and
wanted to ask his way.

As the centuries went
on, human beings came
to see more and more of
each other. Boats were
invented to cross streams
and seas, paths and roads
were constructed to cross
mountains. People slow-
ly found out that where-
ever they saw other men
and women, no matter
what color their skin, or
how they were dressed,
they were the very same
kind of creatures. This is
just a fact, as plain a fact
as that tiny little spar-
rows and great fat hens
belong to the bird family.
We human beings are
all as alike as members
of one family, because
we *are* members of one
family.

So, since the children of one family are all brothers and sisters, you can see that any other human being really is a brother, even though you may never have laid eyes on him before.

It has taken a long time for men and women to grasp this idea clearly enough to think about it. Yet we have for centuries acted on it, coming and going as we do alongside other members of the human family in a street, in a crowd. We are not afraid of them; we don't want to make them afraid of us. We just go about our business, sure of what they are likely to do, as they are sure of us, as none of us would be sure of an entirely different kind of creature, like a polar bear.

But because we don't always remember—or maybe don't even realize definitely—what it is that makes us so act, this article was put first in the Declaration, to remind us of the basis of our human lives.

ARTICLE 2

Everyone is entitled to all the rights and freedoms set forth in this Declaration, without distinction of any kind, such as race, color, sex, language, religion, political or other opinion, national or social origin, property, birth or other status.

Furthermore, no distinction shall be made on the basis of the political, jurisdictional or international status of the country or territory to which a person belongs, whether it be independent, trust, non-self-governing or under any other limitation of sovereignty.

Suppose you were moving into a new place to live, and wanted to get the house which was to be your family's home perfectly clean. It wouldn't be definite enough if, as you were all talking it over together beforehand and making plans, you said only, "We must clean the house."

32

There are so many, many different things in a house which get dirty. You would be much surer of not forgetting any part of what you want done, if you made a list, all of you thinking about it: if you wrote down, "Clean the floor, the walls, the ceiling, the shelves, the steps on the stairs, the floor and steps leading to the front veranda and to the back door, the places where clothes are to be hung, the place in the kitchen where food is to be prepared," and so on.

That's the way Article 2 of the Declaration was written. There was perfect agreement as to what was wanted in it from every single man and woman on the Committee of eighteen who were especially working on the Declaration, and from all those in the big General Assembly of the United Nations. The first part of this Article—"Everyone is entitled to all the rights and freedoms set forth in this

Declaration"—says clearly what they thought, what they all wanted to say. You might think it would have been safe to leave it at that.

But that would have been like a family's saying, "We must clean the house." If nothing more was said, they might work together at cleaning it, and move in; and then, some day, the little door under the stairs might fall open—and there would be a place full of dust and trash and dirt that they had forgotten to clean.

The United Nations wanted to mention by name every single kind of unfairness which in the past had been done to any group of people. They wanted to make sure that nobody would be overlooked in this statement of the rights agreed on by the United Nations as belonging to all.

So they put their heads together to mention all the kinds of people who had ever been shut out from such rights anywhere, so that they could be brought to mind. Men and women have sometimes been excluded from their fair rights and freedoms because of their race, so this was mentioned.

It was a little as though all the delegates to the United Nations stood up and called to the enormous crowd of human beings all around the globe, "Everybody, *no matter what race*, come on out into your fair share of freedom, as big a share as anybody."

Then, just in case the word "race" wasn't definite enough, they said, "Doesn't make any difference what color you are, step out into freedom."

Then, maybe, the women of the world, because for so long and in so many places they have been kept less free than men, might wonder if they too were to have their full human share of freedom. The voice of the Declaration speaks specially to them: "You women, you too, have the right to be as free as any other grownup."

But in many places people who believe in one kind of religion have been shut out from a full place in the freedom-world. They might be asking themselves, uncertainly, "Do you suppose *we* are in this, too?" The voice of the Declaration would ring out, "Yes, you too!"

You can make up for yourselves the reasons for the other definitely named summons to freedom: "You who have little money—you have all the rights we're setting down in this Declaration just as much as if you were ever so rich." "*You*, whose father and mother were—maybe—slaves. Don't think for a minute that that makes you a slave." "*You* who have a lot of property—you haven't any *more* of these great human rights and freedoms than the person who earns just enough each day to make both ends meet. . . . Money hasn't a thing to do with human rights."

The United Nations tried to think of every single kind of person who might have been kept out of his fair share of human rights and freedoms, and to call to them all, "Human freedom is so great an idea, that in it there's room for all!"

When you think of Article 2, listen as if to a big bell ringing out joyously: "There's room for all! There's room for all!"

ARTICLE 3

*Everyone has the right to life,
liberty and security of person.*

Here is an article which hasn't a thing
new in it for any of us. We know it already. We
are used to it. Yet it's well to remind us of it.
Sometimes we forget things just because we are so
used to them.

Suppose when you wake up some morning you
hear a neighbor say that during the night a new
family moved into your village, your town, your
city, the apartment house where you live. That's
all that is known about them—so far. You haven't
heard whether the newcomers are a group of two
or three young sisters living together, or several

elderly brothers, or a father and mother and their children. The person who tells you about them hasn't seen them, so he can't tell you whether they are black, or white, or brown. They may be Mohammedans, or Christians, or Buddhists, or Zoroastrians, or maybe belong to some religion you never heard of. They may have lots of money, or be very poor. For all you know they may be French or Chinese or from Texas.

You might think that you don't know a single thing about them.

But you do. Wherever you live, no matter how you have been brought up, you know something definite about the way you must treat them, before you've even laid eyes on them. You know you must not try to keep them shut up (as long as they act like decent folks who don't harm anybody). You know you must not frighten them, so that they think they are in danger. You know you must give them a fair chance to live and to enjoy life. All this "knowing" is so natural to you that you hardly realize it. You are as sure of it as that both you and the unknown newcomers must have air to breathe. Sometimes we forget about air because it is always there. But when somebody reminds us of it, we say, "Oh, yes, of course." Well, we say "Oh, yes, of course," when we are reminded by this Article that we don't have to be personally acquainted with another human being, or even to have seen him, to know that we have an obligation to respect his life and his freedom. We accept this obligation just because we are human and so is he—the unknown.

We have a right to feel proud of this obligation. It is a comfort to be sure that all of us accept it. There are many things which we human beings do that aren't much to be proud of. But that we have come, through many hundreds and thousands of years, to take for granted what's said in Article 3 —that *is* something encouraging. When we stop to think, it makes us feel that humanity, for all its faults, can step forward toward better ways of living.

ARTICLE 4

No one shall be held in slavery or servitude; slavery and the slave trade shall be prohibited in all their forms.

You WOULDN'T THINK, WOULD YOU, THAT our not knowing something could make us feel especially cheerful. But so it is, when we read this Article. Out of the myriads of human beings on the globe, not many of us have ever seen a slave, a real slave—a human being absolutely belonging to another human being, as a dog or horse belongs.

Because of this, we may feel some surprise that an Article against slavery was thought to be needed.

There are several reasons why the Universal Declaration put in an Article against this great human wrong. One reason is because, alas, there are still, in some places in the world, actual slaves who belong to others, who haven't any rights of their own, just as there were when our great-grandparents lived. As long as one single human being is held in slavery, the rest of us can't be easy in our minds.

The second reason is perhaps not so plain. It is that men and women can be held as slaves even without belonging, like a dog, to a personal owner. Their freedom can be taken away from them by unjust laws, or unjust ways of using the laws.

One kind of slavery might be created this way. Suppose a poor man buys some things he needs. He hasn't money at that time to pay for them, so it is agreed he'll work for the man who sold them, till he has earned enough money to pay his debt. The work is to be done off in the woods, far from any settlement. The man he owes money to provides the food. When he has earned enough to pay the debt, the man who sold the goods says, "Now you are in debt for all those meals you have eaten." So the poor man goes on working to pay his second debt. And he's kept working. No matter how much he earns, he's always told he still hasn't paid all he owes.

Many other ways have been invented to make people really slaves, although not in exactly the same way as they used to be.

None of these ways can last long enough to

create slavery if they are done out in the open, where everybody knows about it and where the poor men can get honest legal advice. That kind of slavery can't go on if everybody in the community is allowed to know about it, because in every community there are people of good will who, if they can talk freely to the poor men, will help them figure what their debts are and whether they have really paid them; or who will provide honest lawyers to protect their legal rights. The only way to keep human beings in this kind of slavery is to keep them out of sight where most people don't know about them—or don't think about it, at least—and where the only ones who see them are those who want to keep them working.

You can see how this particular kind of slavery might be still managed. People who don't care about doing the right thing could think up many other ingenious ways of keeping others out of their fair rights. But they can't if the rest of us know about it.

So, you see, in a Declaration of Human Rights, there's still some reason to have a special article against one of the greatest human wrongs—slavery. Maybe in one form or another, slavery is something we need to keep our eye on, to keep putting down, forbidding, preventing, because in one form or another it keeps coming back.

ARTICLE 5

No one shall be subjected to torture or to cruel, inhuman or degrading treatment or punishment.

THERE ARE SEVERAL GOOD REASONS FOR MAKing this Article part of the Universal Declaration of Human Rights. The greatest reason is plain the minute you read it:—it is wrong, it is wicked to make other people suffer, or to make them feel they are no good. Every human being has a right not to fear that his fellow men will act wickedly toward him. That's the moral reason for this Article, and a mighty one.

There is another reason—a practical commonsense reason. Terrible punishments do not make human beings better, more inclined to do the right thing, more useful to the rest of society. Just the

other way around. We don't get more of what we
need from men and women by inflicting great pain
on them, or making them ashamed of themselves.
We get less.

What *do* we need from our fellow men? We
want them to let others have their fair part in the
good things of life; not to grab more than their
share for themselves; to help with the work that
needs to be done. The many laws and rules made
by courts and schools and fathers and mothers and
governments and judges—every one of them has
the same purpose, to make more sure that people
do the right thing. And we now know that nobody
is helped to do the right thing by being cruelly
hurt, or badly scared, or made to feel that he's no
good.

It was perhaps in training animals not to do
harm and to be useful, that men began to see that
threats and fear and pain are not the surest ways
to teach. For instance, the most skillful trainers
found out that horses can be taught much better
by being made to feel proud and happy when they

do the right thing than by being beaten and hurt and scared when they don't. In fact, horses that are beaten and hurt and scared become either savagely dangerous, or so broken-spirited that they aren't really useful to work.

The same thing is true in teaching children lessons. If a boy makes a mistake in spelling, he doesn't spell better if he is made to write on the blackboard, a hundred times, "I am a fool." It either makes him angry so that he hates the whole idea of learning anything, or so discouraged about himself that it is much harder for him even to try to get his lessons. That's the second reason for Article 5—that nobody learns to do better by being shamed or being badly hurt.

There's a third, dark and ugly reason back of this Article, not as plain to the eye as the other two, but well known to those who understand human nature. It is this: the reason why, in many cases, a person makes other people suffer pain is not at all to help them do better, but to give himself a horrid pleasure, a pleasure that is poison in any human heart.

Do you think that only dreadful people are in danger from this dreadful pleasure? No, it stands close to any one of us, ready to come in if we open the door.

Take such a simple situation as this: some little children are playing together in the sand. You are asked to take care of them for a while, and you promise you will. It looks like an easy job, just to manage them so that they can enjoy their play and get along without quarreling, for an hour or so. But one of them keeps snatching toys away from the others and breaking them. You get very angry with him for spoiling the children's good time. If you get so angry that you lose your head, you're likely to feel like kicking him, or sticking a pin into him, or yelling at him that you'll knock him down if he doesn't stop.

You think it would make *you* feel better to hurt him. Yet you know well enough that if you do, he will either be angry back at you and try to smash a lot more toys, or break down and cry at the top of his voice because he is afraid of you. The others would cry too, be frightened, or excited, or maybe share your ugly pleasure in another's pain. You know that this would prevent you from doing what you said you would do, help the children play peaceably together.

If you could cool off and collect your wits, you'd remember what it was you really meant to do, you'd see that to kick or knock down a child wouldn't help you, and you'd start inventing ways to show the little snatcher how to take turns, how to play fair.

People who make the laws are coming, little by little, to realize that all this is as true of grownups who do wrong, as of children. To give great pain to somebody who has done wrong does not at all make him feel more like doing right.

Of course, his wrongdoing must be stopped, to protect other people. But he needs, just like anybody else, to learn how to play fair, and to be encouraged to think he can. If there is something the matter with his head, so that he can't learn this, he'll have to be kept away from others. But he can be freed, if he does learn that it is possible for him to live with other people without harming them. Not one thing would be gained for him, or for any of us, by frightening him or hurting him badly, or making him too ashamed of himself to try to do better.

Reason number one: it's wrong and wicked to torture other people. Number two: it doesn't do anybody any good. Number three: it does a great deal of harm to those who inflict the pain and to the rest of us who allow it.

ARTICLE 6

*Everyone has the right to recogni-
tion everywhere as a person before
the law.*

THIS ARTICLE SIX IS ONLY THIRTEEN WORDS
long. Yet the idea in it was one of the hardest to
think through accurately, and to express clearly.
You'd never dream what a lot of work and time
went into deciding what everybody thought about
the idea; and then thinking how it could be put
into words. So we too, if we are going to understand it, will have to sit up straight in our chairs
and put our minds to work.

There are two words in it which, if we emphasize them, make the meaning plainer. *"Everyone*
has the right to recognition *everywhere* as a person
before the law."

It has taken a long time for people to realize that all human beings are of the same family. And a longer time still for us all to see that because we are of one human family, every man and every woman, everywhere, is inside the framework of human law.

What does that phrase really mean—"inside the framework of human law"? To answer that question, let us think about what the law is.

Law is not just something printed in big words inside big books, read only by lawyers, shut up within courtrooms, considered by nobody but juries and judges. Laws are no more than the rules invented by human beings to help them get along with each other without quarreling over every little detail, and to help us give everybody as fair a chance as everybody else. We make laws all the time, whenever we put our heads together to get something done. Suppose we wish, just for fun, as part of celebrating a holiday, to have a foot race. Everybody there doesn't get out on his own, start from anywhere, and run in any direction he takes a notion to. That wouldn't be a race, it wouldn't be fun, it wouldn't be anything. So we agree on some laws. They are to regulate just that one race. Such "laws" only last till the end of that race. But as long as the race is on, they are as real as any laws.

The first rule we make is that all runners must start from the same line, marking the beginning of the course. Then we make a rule that no one must begin to run before the others do. He'd have an unfair advantage. Then we agree on a rule that nobody must try to push over or trip up any other runner. This contest is to find out who can run fastest, not who can bother other people most. Then we agree that all the runners must keep going till they get to a line marking the end of the course, so they will all have the same distance to run. Finally we agree that the first runner who gets to the end line shall have a reward—a gold coin, or maybe a red apple.

Suppose, as the runners stand ready, a stranger

comes along and stands toeing the line with the others. We haven't any rule that everybody in the race must live in our town or be personally known to us, so we let him in.

Now, take a long breath and notice that the next sentence is so important it is printed in italics. *The minute he is in the race, all the rules apply to him as much as to all the others.* He must toe the line, he must start on the signal, he must not trip up anybody else, and nobody must trip him up.

If he comes in first, he must have the prize. The judge may be the most important man in town, but he is not allowed to say, as the stranger comes in ahead of the others, "No, you don't live here, so you can't have the reward. I'm going to give the prize to that redheaded runner, back there, because I like his father." No, everybody in that race "is inside the framework of its rules." He must obey them and he must have the same protection they give to others. Article 6 means that no human being is outside the framework of human law.

Suppose a stranger to the town wants to buy a house. All the laws of that place apply to him, although he may never have set foot in the town before. If he makes a first payment and agrees to pay so much every month, the man selling the house can't take his first payment, keep it, and later tell him just to go away. Both the buyer and the seller are inside the framework of the law.

Or suppose he agrees to work for so much a day, and the man who promised to pay him says at quitting time, "No, I don't feel like paying you as much as that." There are laws which regulate the hiring of workers, and each person, stranger or not, is as much protected by them and must as completely obey them as the runner must obey the rules of the foot race and be protected by them.

If you'll bear in mind the "law-rules" about the foot race, if you'll remember that because of them even the judge, no matter what he felt like doing, could not refuse to give the reward to the runner who had obeyed all the rules and run the fastest, you will know the meaning of the phrase, "All human beings are inside the framework of the human law."

ARTICLE 7

All are equal before the law and are entitled without any discrimination to equal protection of the law. All are entitled to equal protection against any discrimination in violation of this Declaration and against any incitement to such discrimination.

IF YOU WILL LOOK BACK AT THE FIRST THREE Articles, you'll see that each one is about a different human right, all three rights great, noble, important, and none of them new to the minds of men and women of good will today. All of them have been recognized, in general, by the best members of our human race. So they are really strong reminders of what we already know to be true about human rights.

Article 1 reminded us that all human beings belong to the same family—the human race.

Article 2 reminded us that everybody, no matter who, so long as he or she is a human being, is entitled to certain general rights. We are not born all exactly alike: some people can sing much better than others, for instance. What Article 2 means is that no matter how different in some ways we are, we are all equal in our right to the freedoms proclaimed in this Declaration.

Article 3 contains another great idea. Everybody should be as free, as sure that he is not going to be attacked or imprisoned, as all other human beings.

But freedom is such an enormous right, that there are a lot of ways of looking at it. A number of the Articles are put in just to remind us that there are many kinds of freedoms, not just one, and that each freedom is the right of every human being—so long as he doesn't harm others.

To begin with, there is bodily freedom. Articles 4 and 5 remind us of human wrongs we must prevent, which keep men and women from being bodily free and protected from hurt. That's the first thing to look out for.

But those who are free to come and go as they like, and not as somebody else orders them to, don't have a fair chance if they don't stand as good a show for being fairly treated in law courts as anybody else. There is a word used in Article 7 which we haven't found before in the descriptions of rights to which human beings are entitled. The word is "protection." Read Article 7 over, and you'll see it twice: "entitled without discrimination to equal protection of the law" and "equal protection against any discrimination in violation of this Declaration. . . ." You might think the same idea is expressed in slightly different ways. But it is not quite the same idea.

For example, suppose two neighbors quarrel over the boundary line between their fields. One of them is a nephew of a judge, and the son of a lawyer. The other one doesn't personally know any lawyer, is not known to the judge. They take their quarrel into a court to have it settled by law. The nephew of the judge shouldn't have any better chance there than anybody else.

Here's another case. I see among the advertisements of "help wanted" one which calls for some kind of work I know how to do. I go to the address, and apply for the job. The man who wants the work done says he'd give me the position all right, except that the business firm he works for has a rule against hiring anybody with curly hair or a dark skin. My hair is curly and my skin is dark. So, even though I could do the work needed as well as anybody, I'm not given a chance at it.

But many countries have a law which forbids an employer to discriminate against anyone just because of the color of his skin or the kind of hair he has. In countries with such a law, I can appeal to a judge and he will give me "protection" against this type of discrimination—that is, he won't allow the quality of my hair to prevent me from earning my living by doing useful work I know how to do.

ARTICLE 8

Everyone has the right to an effec-tive remedy by the competent na-tional tribunals for acts violating the fundamental rights granted him by the constitution or by law.

YOU MIGHT THINK THERE IS NOT VERY MUCH difference between the Articles which follow Article 3, down to Article 13. Article 3 claims for everybody the general right to life, liberty, and security of person. What's the need for those nine Articles which follow, protecting some special freedom or right?

Anybody reading this Declaration hastily might ask himself, "Why isn't Article 3 enough?"

But that Third Committee which wrote this Declaration did not work hastily. For long hours, long days, month after month, eighteen responsible, fine men and women, gathered from eighteen different countries, put their thoughts together about the rights every human being ought to have. They lay awake nights trying to get it all clear in their

own minds. Then they went to the Committee
meeting and listened earnestly to other people's
opinions.

When finally they were sure what the general
opinion was, they had to work just as hard to find
the exact words to express what they wanted to
say. They all wanted, as Mrs. Roosevelt put it, to
make the Declaration "brief, broad, clear." They
wanted it to be short so that everybody could read
it, but they wanted to leave out nothing that needed
to be said. And above all, they wanted the meaning to be clear.

So not a word, not a comma, has been used without a great deal of thought, by people with plenty
of brains who were trying with all their might to
make the Declaration as nearly right as they could.

These Articles (Articles 3 to 13) might be called
the "law articles." Perhaps one reason why the
ordinary reader, when he first looks at them,
doesn't seem to see much difference between them,
is that not many of us need to think often about

laws. Mostly we get along in our everyday lives without appearing in law courts. But the people who wrote the Declaration of Human Rights saw that there is a danger in the very fact that ordinary people don't think much about the laws and don't know much about them.

The history of human law shows that as the centuries go by, the legal system everywhere has a way of growing less and less simple. There is a danger of its becoming so complicated that only a learned

lawyer knows his way around in the courts. But of course many of us who need the protection of the law are not as learned as lawyers. Article 8 claims that every single human being is entitled to some sure way of getting his legal rights that is simple enough, direct enough, and understandable enough to be used by anybody who needs it.

Suppose one of us is being kept from voting at an election by some no-good people who say they'll kill him if he tries to vote. He knows that he has a right to the protection of the law of his country.

But, starting out from his home to look for such protection, he asks himself, "Which way do I go?"

Article 8 means to remind everybody that he should know which direction to take to get in touch with those charged with making the laws work. He has the right to know this, as much as anybody has the right to know which direction to take to get to safety in case of a fire in the building he is in.

Of course in each different country, each region, sometimes even each city, the way to reach out for legal protection may be different. But the principle is the same. Everybody has the right to be protected by law from injustice. If you don't know how to make a quick start to get this protection, it is your duty as a citizen to keep looking, to keep claiming and insisting on this right for you, for everybody.

ARTICLE 9

No one shall be subjected to arbitrary arrest, detention or exile.

Here is another "legal article." It is short, the words in it are simple, there is only one sentence in it. Yet to understand its purpose takes some thought. Not, of course, a tenth part—even a hundredth part—as much thought as the writers of the Declaration gave to it. But much more than one needs to understand an ordinary sentence with just as many words in it, such as, "I went out to the market today and bought some food." You take one look at such a sentence and you know everything in it.

But to see what is really in those few words of Article 9, you need to read slowly, to think, to know something about the human past, maybe to talk it over with other people who genuinely care about getting fair play for everybody.

The part of the human past you need to know is this: Centuries ago, those who wanted to grab more than their share of the good things of life invented a way to keep other people from interfering with their grabbing. They found out that if they wanted to put somebody they didn't like into prison, one way to manage this was to send some armed men, paid by them, to carry him off. Once he was shut up in a cell, it was impossible for him to do anything about it, and it was very hard for his friends to help him.

Those who kept him in prison could say, and did say, that he had been arrested because he had done something wrong. If, then, his friends said he must have a fair trial, his enemies could say that he was going to be brought to trial for his crime in a regular law court, where his friends could help defend him. But they just wouldn't have the trial. They'd keep putting it off. They'd keep him locked up in his cell.

Unless his family and friends could collect more armed men than those who guarded the prison, and have a big fight with them, and break down the door to the cell, they couldn't get to him and he couldn't get out.

The history of our human race is often discouraging to good people. But there's one encouraging thing about it. A great many times it has happened, when something wrong goes on for a long time, that men and women put their heads together and "do something about it." They just take hold of the wrong and make it right. That's what happened about this kind of unjust arrest, this unlawful imprisonment of a man without letting him have a chance to defend himself legally. The law was changed. Laws can be changed, and this one was. First in one, then in several, then in many countries, it was seen to cause an injustice. So it was made over. A number of nations now make it illegal to arrest a person and shut him up in prison, without giving him the right to see a judge immediately and to tell his side of the story to a serious, responsible legal authority, whose business it is to see that the prisoner has fair play.

To make that right reach out over all the world was the purpose of Article 9. And while they were about it, a statement was added about another right of the same sort—the right not to be sent away from your own country without having a chance to see if the law will let you stay.

We have seen that in many of these Articles, the general meaning comes out more clearly if you know what word to emphasize. In Article 9 the

word to say most loudly is "arbitrary." We can't
claim the right never to be arrested. Anybody who
burns down a neighbor's house or steals his money
should be arrested. That's according to law, and
good law. What Article 9 is saying is that no one
shall be arrested *except according to the law,* and
that includes a chance to speak up for himself—
not to the armed men who did the arresting, but
in a quiet law court, before a fair judge who wants
to do the right thing and who is trained to know
what the right thing is, according to law.

ARTICLE 10

Everybody is entitled in full equality to a fair and public hearing by an independent and impartial tribunal, in the determination of his rights and obligations and of any criminal charge against him.

H‍ERE'S A BIG BOY, TWELVE OR THIRTEEN YEARS old, throwing a ball. Nearly all big boys, everywhere, practice throwing balls. Maybe this is a basketball, or a soccer ball, and the boy who's practicing with it wants to learn how to play well enough to be on a team. Maybe it is homemade, stuffed with bran or cornhusks, and he's getting ready for a game to be played with bigger boys. Maybe a prize has been offered for the boy who can best hit a mark with a ball. Anyhow, he has picked out a good place to practice, and there he is, thinking about nothing but how to throw his ball. Off to one side, a group of young mothers are sitting in the sun, mending clothes and keeping an eye on their children playing jackstones and jumping rope near by.

All of a sudden a little boy, just old enough to begin to run around, dashes off and runs in front of the big boy. The ball hits him on the shoulder and knocks him down.

He begins to scream at the top of his lungs. His mother flings down her mending and rushes towards him. A couple of men going by stop to say angrily to the big boy, "Aren't you ashamed to knock down a poor little fellow like that!" All the children stop their play and come swarming around, pushing and shouting. One of the passers-by sees that there is a policeman on the corner, and runs to tell him to come to arrest the big boy.

Something like this might happen, you see, to anybody.

What do *you* think should happen next?

It would be hard on the big boy if he were left just to the mother who, of course, is frantic at the idea that somebody has been attacking her poor little son; to the two men who say they saw the big boy knock the little fellow down; and to the policeman, who wasn't there at all. The boy who was throwing the ball really has a good many things he could bring out to defend himself, but if the only people to listen to him were those right around him when it happened, he would not have any chance at all to be believed. If he could get to other people, he might ask his teacher in school to tell about the reason why he was practicing with a ball. The neighbors on his street would be willing to say that he has little brothers and sisters and is always good to them. If the other mothers were to be asked

what they knew about it, and if they'd had time to cool off, they would have to say that he had been practicing with that ball, day after day, and had never thrown it anywhere near anybody. The two passers-by, if they were quietly questioned as to just what they had really seen, would say that they had not noticed what the big boy was doing, until the little boy fell down. The policeman would admit that he himself hadn't seen a thing.

If the matter were laid before some honest, sensible people, in a calm, reasonable way, all these facts would certainly come out. But not if the boy had to defend himself from those excited people, while the small child went on screaming more and more loudly as he saw how sorry everybody was for him.

The only persons who can put their whole minds on a tangle like that, and honestly try to find out what happened, are honest, intelligent people who haven't already gone off half-cocked without knowing all the facts. These people must be known to be fair and square. They must have good brains, too, and they must have had some practice in trying to unravel what the truth is, from what is said by different witnesses.

If the ball-throwing boy has a chance to tell his side of the story to such a group, he'll get fair play. Not otherwise.

ARTICLE 11

(1) Everyone charged with a penal offense has the right to be presumed innocent until proved guilty according to law in a public trial at which he has had all the guarantees necessary for his defense.

(2) No one shall be held guilty of any penal offense on account of any act or omission which did not constitute a penal offense, under national or international law, at the time when it was committed. Nor shall a heavier penalty be imposed than the one that was applicable at the time the penal offense was committed.

DID YOU EVER HAPPEN TO THINK HOW IMPOSSIBLE it is to prove—absolutely prove—that you did *not* do something? Suppose you walked into a house and found a beautiful vase lying on the floor, broken to bits. If the owner came in and said angrily that you had broken it, how could you *prove* that you hadn't?

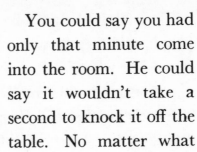

You could say you had
only that minute come
into the room. He could
say it wouldn't take a
second to knock it off the
table. No matter what
you said, he could keep saying, "Well, you *could*
have done it." And all you could reply is, "The
fact that I could doesn't show I *did*."

If you never thought about this before, it may be
a new idea to you that it is possible to get proof
that somebody *did* a thing, but that nobody can
prove that he *didn't*. But it really is a very old
idea. Hundreds of years ago men found it to be
true, and made a rule that it isn't right to say that
somebody has done something wrong, unless there
is proof of it.

But we must all watch out that the proof is
really true. Suppose that as you stepped in and
looked down astonished at that broken vase, the
owner should come out of the next room, shut the
door behind him, and shout, "Now I've got you!
Inside that room, I have proof that you broke
that."

You'd have a right to tell him, "You bring what
you *say* is proof right out in the open, and let
people hear it and make up their minds whether
it's any good or not."

There should always be a chance for fair-minded people who aren't part of the quarrel themselves to see just what facts are being given and to decide about whether they really are proofs.

Here's another case: suppose a home or a school wants to try to keep the floors of its rooms clean. A new rule is made—anybody who doesn't clean off his shoes before he comes in, must sweep all the floors. That's fair. But if you had brought mud in on your shoes two weeks before the rule was voted, it wouldn't be fair to make you sweep the floors. If there wasn't any rule at the time you forgot to brush off your shoes, you didn't break any rule. In the same way, suppose the rule gets changed, so that those who bring in dirt must scrub the floors as well as sweep them. If somebody had been careless about brushing off his shoes before the change in the rule was made, it wouldn't be fair to make him do the scrubbing. This is so simple that any child, even a little boy or girl just beginning school, could understand it.

ARTICLE 12

No one shall be subjected to arbitrary interference with his privacy, family, home or correspondence, nor to attacks upon his honor and reputation. Everyone has the right to the protection of the law against such interference or attacks.

T HE IDEA IN THIS ARTICLE IS NOT LIKE THOSE which go before it, nor those which follow. From Article 3 to this Article 12, the statements have been that everybody has a right not to be hurt by others, not to be shut up in prison (if he has not done any harm), not to be unfairly treated in law courts, and so on. That is, they say that society must not harm the individual man or woman.

After this Article 12, another idea is expressed in various ways; that society should not only refrain from hurting men and women, but should help them to be free to do certain things—to vote, to move around from one place to another, to earn their livings by work, to call in a doctor when they are sick, and so on.

Article 12 is different. It does not claim that men and women should be protected from bad treatment from others; it does not remind us that we should help each other—it states the right of each human being to have a certain amount of no treatment at all from others—to be let alone.

This right to be let alone doesn't sound as important as it is, even when you use a dictionary word and call it "the right to privacy." We don't often think about this right to have things *not* happen to you. Perhaps because it is hard to make a picture in one's mind of things which don't happen.

Let's think of it from the other end. If you were starting to grow a plant in your room, and wished to make a list of all the things you ought to do for it, to have it grow strong, flower, and go to seed, what items would you put down in the list? You'd say, wouldn't you, that you should provide good soil for the plant's roots, put it where it would get enough sunshine, give it enough water, and keep the room not too hot and not too cold.

Would that be enough? No, that list would have in it everything you must do, but there is something you must *not* do which is just as important— you must not let other plants crowd it too closely. It needs to have enough space around it to grow in, just as much as it needs food, water, sunlight.

And so do men and women and children.

A human being's health and growth depend on good food, safety from attack, a chance to work at something worth doing, medical care in sickness—and also on having elbow room. He can't grow, he can't develop, he can't become what the best in him might be, without a certain amount of being let alone, of privacy.

If you knew that a letter you are writing to a dear friend is going to be read by a stranger, you wouldn't write it at all as you would if your friend were going to be the only one to see it. The letter you would like to write him just never gets into words. And when you receive a letter from a member of your family, even if there is nothing secret or specially personal in it, you don't like to have the people around you crowd close to read it over your shoulder. It isn't only that you want to keep

them from knowing what's in it. They couldn't get the real meaning of what's in it, even if they forced you to let them read the words. To understand it, they would need to know the person who wrote the letter, to know what you think of each other, to know what you have said to each other in the past. You know all that, and so you get the true message of the letter. They wouldn't understand it, no matter how many times they read the words in it.

Imagine a person in your room with you, watching every single thing you do, asking you why you do that, asking you why you don't do something different, commenting on the answers you give. Even though you might not have anything you wanted to hide from him, how you would hate to have him there! How relieved you would be when he went away and you could close the door and begin to act like yourself.

Suppose you had kept a diary for a while, to write down your special thoughts and feelings. It might not have any secrets in it, but how you would hate to have a stranger find it and read it aloud to other strangers.

The right of every person to have enough elbow room to think things out for himself without anybody's interfering; the right of every family to solve its own problems and have its own kind of

good times together without the neighbors' looking in through the windows at them any minute and misunderstanding what they see; the right of everyone to say just what he feels in a letter to one other person who will know what he means—the right just to be let alone is one of the important human rights.

There is another idea in this Article that is worth thinking about. Not only should each one of us have the right to be let alone, and the right to talk or correspond privately with our friends, we also should have the right to protection from people who keep saying untrue and disagreeable things about us. It is astonishing how careless or unkind men or women enjoy mean gossip, like to pass along a made-up story which makes a friend seem worse than he is. Of course, people have the right to judge others for what they are, for what they say and believe and do. But nobody has the right to spread lies about others.

In most countries, there are already laws against slander and libel and there should be, everywhere, as Article 12 says. But even good laws are not enough. We should all help prevent mean, malicious, exaggerated gossip. It is not always easy to trace down the rumor. Some people find ways of sneaking around behind a law and harming somebody's reputation by lies. We should all feel responsibility to help protect the freedom of Article 12. Like many other of our rights and freedoms, this is one that can't be enforced altogether even by the best laws. We are personally needed—every one of us—to stand guard over other people's right to privacy, if we hope to have our own personal lives free from other people's pushing in on us.

We should be thankful that the Declaration speaks up for this great freedom from interference with our privacy along with other human freedoms.

ARTICLE 13

(1) Everyone has the right to freedom of movement and residence within the borders of each State.

(2) Everyone has the right to leave any country, including his own, and to return to his country.

DID YOU EVER SEE A PERSON WHO LIKES TO sit up straight, trying to sit in a chair meant for people who like to lean back? He sits on the edge of the seat, uncomfortably balanced, till his back gets tired; then he tries to lean back a *little,* can't manage it, twists himself forward again. He looks miserable and makes everybody around him restless.

If only he could move over into a straight-backed chair, the right shape for him, he'd sit quietly.

Or maybe you've seen the opposite—somebody who loves to lean back, trying to sit on a chair with an up-and-down back. He too sprawls and twists and drives everybody around him distracted. It's not his fault. It's not their fault. One chair is not better than another chair. It's just that all chairs don't fit the same people.

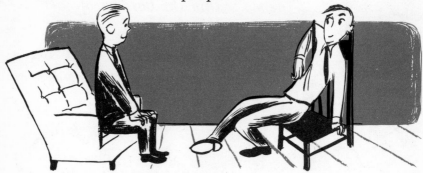

Different parts of your country are like different chairs—some suit one kind of person, some suit another. If you are not in the one that is right for you, or if the ways of earning your living in another place would be more to your taste, what harm do you do by moving around? None. If you do find what you like, you settle down, you're happier, you work better and get more useful things done, and you won't bother the people around you.

But we all make mistakes. Suppose after you've moved into another part of your country, or of the big world, you think, "Well, after all, now I see the way other people manage their lives, I prefer the way I was born to." Then you should be free to move back where you started from, because now you have found that it really is the right place for you.

Some of the greatest advances in the human world have come because people did not want to stay where they were born and brought up, and went to live in some other country. Sometimes they moved because they wanted a chance to do something special, not needed in the old home-region, very useful somewhere else. Think of the splendid farmers who came to the United States from Europe, because there was much more room in America to make land useful to humanity. What a loss it would have been if they had not been allowed to leave their crowded home country-sides.

Men and women learn from each other. The chances to learn the best skills humanity knows are much greater when everybody can go and come freely, taking along with them all they have learned at home, ready to show others new ways of managing life.

In the days since the war, there has been another great movement of people, some escaping from persecution, some from war and the threat of war, some in search of a better life. Article 13, when it says that people have the right to leave any country including their own, and, if they want to, to return to their own country, is helping along that chance to learn from each other which is one of our best human hopes.

ARTICLE 14

(1) Everyone has the right to seek and to enjoy in other countries asylum from persecution.

(2) This right may not be invoked in the case of prosecutions genuinely arising from nonpolitical crimes or from acts contrary to the purposes and principles of the United Nations.

M OST OF THESE ARTICLES ARE IDEAS SO GREAT, so broad that they are permanent truths. It is possible to think of them as being hundreds of years from now just as true, just as important for human beings to think about as they are today.

But Article 14 is one which we can all hope will, in the future, need to be explained to readers of the Declaration.

You can imagine, perhaps, a student, two or three centuries from now, getting to the Universal Declaration in his textbook on the development of human ideas about what is fair and right. Everything he reads will seem clear and understandable to him. He'll agree with all the ideas and see why they were stated, because he has lived in a country ruled by these ideas all his life.

But Article 14—he will get stuck on that one. "Asylum from persecution"—what does that mean? Perhaps if he is still young enough to be in a class with a teacher, he will ask about it. The teacher will probably say, "Look down at the bottom of the page. You'll find a footnote explaining it."

Sure enough, there, in fine print, he will read something like this (in textbook language):

"At a certain time in the history of mankind, scientific research had fully proved that all human beings belong to the same family. Learned men who studied the question and made all kinds of tests in scientific laboratories found absolutely no biological difference between human beings from one race to another. Men and women and children, everywhere, need the same food elements for their health, are subject to the same diseases. In all races, some individuals are especially gifted and brainy, some are not so very bright.

"As people in one part of the world came to know more about how other people lived, it was noted as one of the many ways in which human beings are alike, that children everywhere play about the same games. The children in China had no idea what American children did to amuse themselves, yet of their own accord, Chinese boys played shinney, fox and geese, tag, and hide-and-seek. They knew how to fly kites and they played every kind of ball game children of other countries played. One scientist put it this way:

" 'Biologically, all men are brothers. Physiology knows no racial or national boundaries. The desire for activity is as natural for the child of Korea as

it is for the boy or girl in England. The Spanish boy or girl has the same urge to jump and climb, to run and throw, to lift and hang, that causes the American child to do these things.'

"Scientifically trained people, and those who kept track of the discoveries proved in laboratories, knew about this similarity of all human beings to each other. But there were people without much acquaintance with scientifically proved truths, who had the strange idea that the so-called races of mankind were really different from each other. In psychological laboratories where men of learning with the right kind of equipment were seriously studying these facts, it was discovered that there are great innate differences between human individuals, but not between races.

"In a report to the United Nations in 1951, a group of celebrated psychologists, representing many of the nations of the world, stated that 'it has never been possible to separate numbers of two peoples on the basis of mental capacity as they often can be separated on a basis of skin color, hair, and so forth.' In other words, there can be inferior and superior individuals, not superior or inferior races; disagreeable individuals, not disagreeable races."

The student might not see what in the world this had to do with Article 14, and might find it pretty dull reading. But his teacher would say "Go on. You won't get the point until you read it all through, and learn about witches."

So he would read on: "In the middle years of the twentieth century, these facts, although established by scientific research, were not yet universally recognized, and whole groups of certain races were persecuted with the mistaken notion that people are alike in personality and character, if they are alike in such details as color of hair and skin, shape of features, and so on. Just before the date of the organization of the United Nations and the writing of the Universal Declaration of Human Rights, there had been so much persecution of certain racial groups that it was thought best to have a separate Article concerned with this subject.

"Such persecutions were based on ideas as untrue and as widely held by ignorant people, as the earlier persecutions of women thought to be witches. (Elsewhere in this text notice accounts of such witchcraft delusions in the sixteenth and seventeenth centuries.)"

The student would probably think, "I'd better take notes on this. Such ideas sound so foolish, they'll be hard to remember. If I don't write all this down, I'll forget it before examination."

So he'll put down in his notes, "Persecution of

women thought to be witches, sixteenth and seventeenth centuries. Persecution of certain human groups thought to be all the same because of similar color of hair, shape of features, etc. . . ." "Now what was the date when that happened? Oh yes, about the middle of the twentieth century."

Isn't it wonderful to look forward to a time when both kinds of mistakes—persecution of witches, persecution of races—will be so completely forgotten that people won't ever hear about them except in their history textbooks?

Meanwhile we are living in the twentieth century. And people, driven out of their homes by persecution, are looking for a place to settle where they will be safe. That is the meaning of asylum. Read this Article 14 along with Article 13. Some of those people wanting to leave their country in Article 13 are the same people who are looking for asylum in Article 14. And they have the right to do both. Moreover, when they have found asylum they have the right to stay there and enjoy a safe life.

ARTICLE 15

(1) *Everyone has the right to a nationality.*

(2) *No one shall be arbitrarily deprived of his nationality nor denied the right to change his nationality.*

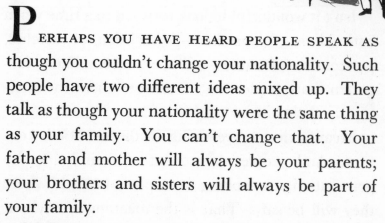

PERHAPS YOU HAVE HEARD PEOPLE SPEAK AS though you couldn't change your nationality. Such people have two different ideas mixed up. They talk as though your nationality were the same thing as your family. You can't change that. Your father and mother will always be your parents; your brothers and sisters will always be part of your family.

Well, when you come to think of it, the human race is like a family. You'll always be human, no matter what! There are disadvantages in being human, and maybe, sometimes, you feel that it would be less bother and more fun to be something else—a fox, a tiger, or a lively skipping squirrel. But you can't! You'll always be human, as long as you live, and other men and women and children will always be your sisters and brothers in humanity. You might as well make up your mind to this, because that's the nature of things. In all the millions of years man has been on the earth, everybody born human has stayed human all his life long. There wasn't anything else he could be.

But not one of us belongs now to the same nationality his forefathers belonged to thousands of years ago. All those ancient, ancient nationalities have turned into something else. You see, nationalities are *not* in the nature of things. They are just inventions made up by men and women. They are like different homes in the same town. Everybody has to have a house to live in, yes. It would be hard on anybody not to have any shelter at all against the weather. But there are many different kinds of shelter. Maybe you like one kind of a house more than another kind. Why shouldn't you live in the one you like best and that suits you best, and let other people live where, and as, *they* like best? It wouldn't do anybody any harm. You'd all still be living in the same town with your human brothers and sisters, although not under the same roof. You'd be right there to rush out if anybody's house caught on fire, to help put out the flames, even if, as far as *you* go, you'd rather live in the one across the street.

A great many people of today want to belong to a country of their own, more than anything else. As a result of war, hundreds of thousands of people now have no nationality. They are called "stateless persons." They are really like people without a roof over their heads.

The United Nations, first through UNRRA and then through the International Refugee Organization, has helped hundreds of thousands of displaced persons many of whom were "stateless." Homes were found for them, but most important of all they were given a chance to gain a new nationality to take the place of the one they had lost.

This is why Article 15 is such an important one. It holds out hope to a great many fine, useful people in our world who need the protection of a country of their own, that protection which we often forget about because we have always had it.

ARTICLE 16

(1) Men and women of full age, without any limitation due to race, nationality or religion, have the right to marry and found a family. They are entitled to equal rights as to marriage, during marriage and at its dissolution.
(2) Marriage shall be entered into only with the free and full consent of the intending spouses.
(3) The family is the natural and fundamental group unit of society and is entitled to protection by society and the State.

GOOD MARRIAGES MEAN GOOD HOMES, AND good homes help every one of us, whether we live in that particular home or not. Children who are brought up in good homes grow up with their various personal good qualities strengthened and developed, full of the ability to enjoy natural, normal life, and with good will towards all.

91

A marriage has a much better chance to be a
good and happy one when both the man and the
woman, the husband and the wife, feel free to
marry or not as they decide, and can choose a mate
who suits their personal needs and tastes. They
are the ones who will have to get along with each
other. They are more apt to be able to live with
satisfaction in marriage if they have chosen each
other freely. If they are not contented in their marriage, they can't make such a good home around
them.

They need all the strength and contentment and
happiness in marriage they can have, to learn how
to carry well the great and beautiful responsibility

for keeping their home cheerful and well-ordered, for training their children to be helpful to others and to be strong and intelligent and happy.

There are many ways of preventing both men and women from feeling really free to marry as they wish. Some of the barriers are set up by actual laws; some by narrow ideas people in their communities have; some by special notions their parents may have. This Article 16 reminds us that marriages and homes are so important to us that there should be as few barriers as possible to freedom of choice in a mate. To be married is to enter into a relation so personal and so permanent, on which so much human happiness and health depends, that the man and woman in it need to make their own decisions about what mate they choose to share life with.

Perhaps, since women have, in the past, found more barriers before them than men, to making a free marriage, and to being equal in marriage, something should be said, specially, about the need for women to be strong and vital and free in marriage.

We human beings all have two legs. And we walk, or run, or climb, ever so much better if they are both equal. We're sorry for anybody who has one leg that's weaker than the other. He limps along very slowly and clumsily, compared to somebody who strides off briskly, his two strong legs taking him, *one,* two, *one,* two, wherever he wants to go. Doctors tell us, too, although we wouldn't think of this, that many pains in the back or bad headaches come from one leg being shorter or weaker than the other.

Now marriage is always made up of two parts, two halves, a man and a woman. They share what has to be done, just as everybody's two legs share in the effort of moving around. And it is just as true of the two parts of marriage as of our two human legs, that things go better if both parts are equally strong, elastic, and vigorous. To try to keep one half of a marriage—the woman —out of some of the rights all human beings have just because they are human, is a little as though we tied up one leg to make its muscles stiffer and weaker than the other one. We couldn't get along at all well that way. We need them both. Nature gave us the two of them. There's no sense to our trying to keep one of them less strong and hence less useful than it might be.

Even when everybody in our human communities is as strong and capable as possible, it is a tremendous undertaking to keep human society going. The more weak and underdeveloped people there are, the harder the strong ones have to work, because they must do more than their share. A good many sensible people begin, like the doctors, to think that some of the troubles human society has, that are like backaches or headaches for individual people, come from trying to keep one half of humanity—women, who are half of every marriage—weaker, less well-trained, more helpless, less able to do half of what needs to be done.

If the woman's half of marriage is kept by laws or by a foolish public opinion from being as strong and brave and capable as the man's half, it makes things harder all around—not just for women, but for everybody.

With so much that must be done to make human life decent and clean and safe and enjoyable, we haven't any too much good will and strength and brains if we get the good of all that everybody can develop—men, women, boys, and girls.

ARTICLE 17

(1) Everyone has the right to own property alone as well as in association with others.

(2) No one shall be arbitrarily deprived of his property.

Y OU KNOW THAT THE chair or cushion or mat you sit on in your parents' home belongs to them, just to them and not to anybody else. Did you ever think as you step out into the streets, or go across a bridge, that bridges and streets belong to your father and mother too? Not just to them alone, but to them along with other people. For if a lot of people didn't work on the street or bridge, and get paid for working, there wouldn't be any street or bridge. If your parents have either worked on it, or paid taxes to pay others who do work on it, why, it is partly their property.

Everywhere there are these two kinds of property. There are two kinds inside your own home as well as outside in the community. Your own shirt, your own hair ribbon, your own toothbrush— they are yours, just yours. The cooking pots and pans, the furniture, the pictures, belong to all the family. If they can't be used by everybody, they are no good to anybody. Suppose you took the cooking things and the furniture into your room, shut the door, and kept everybody outside. You couldn't do anything with those things, and the rest of the family couldn't either. By trying to keep them to yourself you make them no good to anybody.

It's by a natural right that everybody has a share of what everybody needs to use, as well as to the things—like his toothbrush or his clothes—that nobody else uses. When you stop to think about it, we all, no matter where we live, own a part in so many different kinds of property, we can hardly count them up—roads, bridges, schools, hospitals, museums, and so on.

At school there are also things that you own "in association with others" like a swing or a place to play ball. If you push a schoolmate out of the swing, if you never give him a chance to throw his ball on the playground, you're taking away from him something he has as much right to as to his own pencil or his special book or his jacket or his shoes.

It's only quite small children who haven't learned that it's not fair to snatch away from others what belongs to them. Older children don't always *do* what's fair, nor grownups either. People, as well as children, sometimes snatch, sometimes push to keep others out of what belongs to everybody. But we all know better. We know we shouldn't, and this Article 17 is meant to remind us clearly of what everybody with ordinary sense knows already.

ARTICLE 18

Everyone has the right to freedom of thought, conscience and religion; this right includes freedom to change his religion or belief, and freedom, either alone or in community with others and in public or private, to manifest his religion or belief in teaching, practice, worship and observance.

IN THE INTRODUCTION IS SET DOWN THE STORY of the first meeting of peoples from all around the globe, who represented the religions of the world.

They found that, although their beliefs were not the same, they did have the same ideas about what is the right way for human beings to treat each other. Not a single one among all those different religions taught its believers that it is right to steal from others; to treat sick and old people unkindly; to kill others; to take children's food away from them; or to make others work without the rest they need.

This agreement about what is the right way for us to act towards our fellow men and women was not just an idea of those noble leaders. Everybody, everywhere has the same convictions, even those who do take away from others what belongs to them, who do neglect the sick or treat old people badly, and all the rest. They know, every human being knows, that they are doing wrong, not right. But there is a great deal more for human beings to think about than the right way to treat each other. There is the enormous question of why we exist at all. There is the wonder about the relation of our little Earth to all the rest of the vast universe. Can we find out *why* we all agree on what is right and what is wrong to do? What happens to human beings after we die? What should we feel towards one or another of the noble figures who have at different times lived among us, setting us examples of pure, beautiful goodness?

What you think about such great mysteries is your religion. And there is no agreement among human beings as to the answers to those tremendous questions. Yet long experience of human life has taught us all to agree on one fact about religious beliefs. It is this: *they cannot be changed by force or violence.*

They can be changed, and often are changed, by serious thinking, by studying, by growing wiser as to the deep meaning of our life, by listening to what others have to say, by a person's coming into contact with a religion which he loves and believes the minute he hears about it.

But nobody ever saw a person's religious belief changed just because he was threatened with death or pain if he didn't change it.

Nobody's *belief* about anything can be changed by force, not even geography beliefs. People who have never been to school, and young children who haven't yet studied geography, have no idea that the world is round. They can see for themselves that it is flat, and so they believe it is flat. If they were told they would be beaten or killed if they didn't believe the earth to be round like a globe, all they could do would be to lie about it and say they had changed, although they hadn't. In their inner minds, they would still go on believing what seems true to them.

If they were badly enough scared, they would keep still about this, they would take care never to mention it to a soul, they would try not to think about it. But as long as they didn't know with their minds more than what they could see with their eyes, they couldn't imagine that such a strange thing could be true as that what looks perfectly flat, could really be the shape of a ball. It wouldn't seem possible to them, and human minds cannot believe anything to be true which doesn't seem possible, any more than fishes can fly or birds live under water. All force can do is to make them pretend that they believe something to be true which they can't really believe.

So, although they greatly differed among themselves about their religious beliefs, all the representatives of those different faiths voted "Yes" to the idea that everybody has the right to believe what he really does believe, and then to change his belief if, as he lives and grows, his spiritual insight becomes deeper and finer.

ARTICLE 19

Everyone has the right to freedom of opinion and expression; this right includes freedom to hold opinions without interference and to seek, receive and impart information and ideas through any media and regardless of frontiers.

DID YOU EVER HEAR THAT OF ALL THE BILLIONS of snowflakes which in cold climates fall through the air every winter, no two have ever been found exactly alike? It's hard to believe. But scientists on whose word we can rely, tell us that this is true.

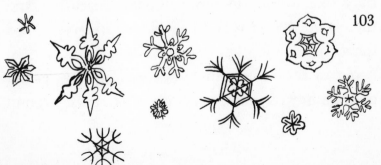

What is more, they tell us that no two of the thousands of leaves on any tree are precisely the same in shape, and size, and color. And we all know that different kinds of trees have leaves quite different from each other.

Doctors who have had a lot of experience taking care of men and women and children, say the same thing about human bodies. No two are precisely the same.

We are beginning to see that this is true of human personalities. No two human minds have precisely the same thoughts about the life around us, no two people feel exactly the same about what they like to eat, to wear, to do, to learn. And there's no reason why they should pretend to feel the same.

Yet of course in many ways, and up to a certain point, many of us are very much like those around us. Nearly every young person likes candy; but not every single one. Nearly everybody likes lively stories. But there *are* people, like the great Einstein, who would rather read a book on science.

To make a law that every single young person should eat just so much candy every day would be foolish for two reasons: (1) most of them will do their best to get candy anyhow without any law; and (2) if you clamp down with that law on every single young person, you'd be forcing some to eat what they don't want, and you wouldn't be making candy any easier to get for those who do want it. There's nothing gained by trying to make those with scientific minds read nothing but love stories, for those who enjoy love stories read nothing but books on higher mathematics.

To try to make everybody think alike—well, you couldn't, anyhow; we all know that. But even if you could, it would be too bad. What would you think of a rule that every single tree in our forests must have leaves the same shape as the oak leaves? The only way you could do this would be to cut down every one of all the different kinds of trees except the oaks. How much poorer we would all be if that were done!

Different kinds of trees, different kinds of human personalities, bear different kinds of fruits. It's not a pity—it's splendid—that there are many kinds of minds and hearts and gifts among human beings. This variety is wealth. It is a rich part of what we are born into.

ARTICLE 20

(1) Everyone has the right to freedom of peaceful assembly and association.
(2) No one may be compelled to belong to an association.

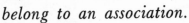

Many of the animals are bigger and stronger than human beings. You might think they could get along much better than we. But they don't.

We don't grow fur to keep us warm like bears. We haven't great claws like tigers. A long line of men holding onto a rope could be pulled off their feet by one elephant. We human beings can't live under water like fishes. Eagles have much sharper eyes than ours. The stupidest dog can smell better than the brightest man or woman. But we can do something which is worth ever so much more than fur or claws or eagle-sharp eyes or great muscles. *We can work constructively together.*

One man alone might not be strong enough to bridge even a brook. But he could get other men to help him. A dozen men could make quite a big bridge, and a hundred people could open the way across a wide river. The tiger could make a meal out of any one of those men. But not in a thousand years could he get other tigers to work with him to make something they need. You can't even imagine tigers working together. This human ability is the best tool we have, so we'd better take good care of it and not let it get dull or broken.

We can't take care of anything unless we understand which part of it is the really useful part. A
man who had never used an ax might think he was
taking good care of it if he kept the handle shiny
with varnish or bright with paint. But the important part of an ax is the cutting edge of the steel.
The important part of this great ability of ours is
to use our *human* qualities in working together, not
just our bodily strength, for we haven't nearly as
much of that kind of strength as horses or mules.
Our working together gets its special value when
everybody on the job uses his brains, ingenuity, and
willingness to cooperate, as well as his strength.

All the special value of that human tool of ours
would be lost if the work were done under the
orders of one or a few men, who had some way to
force the crowd to obey them as if they were animals or machines.

Our *human* strength comes in when we all wish to get the work done and wish to help each other. Any job is much better done when those working have had a chance to help choose what's to be done and to help plan how to do it. Only when they have worked together from the beginning in this way, have they had a chance to join their finest human qualities with those of their fellow men. Hence an important part of getting work well done begins long before anybody picks up a shovel or a compass or a saw or an engineer's slide rule or any other actual tool. The beginning is when men or women talk over a plan together, find out what they all want and agree on it, discuss how to divide the task up, and settle on the place to work and which tools to use.

The only way a group of people can make plans is by getting together to talk things over, by "assembling" freely, as often as needed, so that everybody can have a chance to contribute whatever he can in sound judgment or good will or inventiveness. Even if we do no more than shout, "Hurrah! that's the way to do it!" when somebody has a good plan; or call out, "Take care, maybe that won't work," to a doubtful idea, we will have helped in the planning. Many times, just silently dropping a vote into a ballot box is the same thing as shouting, "Hurrah!" or, "It won't work."

But if somebody doesn't like the idea proposed and doesn't want it to be a success, you won't get any helpful inventiveness or good will from him if you force him to join the group that's making plans. You can force a man to dig with a shovel, but you can't force him to be inventive and ingenious.

We couldn't get anything important done, we couldn't even keep the things we have in running order, if we didn't often and freely meet in groups to talk things over, to compare our ideas, to put our heads together, to profit by other people's brains and willingness to cooperate, which are our specially human qualities.

So keep your eye on the right to hold meetings— all kinds of meetings—and don't let anybody prevent us from getting together.

ARTICLE 21

(1) Everyone has the right to take part in the government of his country, directly or through freely chosen representatives.

(2) Everyone has the right of equal access to public service in his country.

(3) The will of the people shall be the basis of the authority of government; this will shall be expressed in periodic and genuine elections which shall be by universal and equal suffrage and shall be held by secret vote or by equivalent free voting procedure.

Most of the Articles in this Declaration are about human rights—rights which men and women are entitled to just because they are born members of the big human family. None of the rights are new. But some of them had never been agreed on before by people representing such a great number of the nations of the world. Many of them had never before even been talked over by people from such very different kinds of countries.

But Article 21 isn't a bit new. The right it describes has been talked over in all kinds of meetings in all kinds of countries, long before the United Nations was even dreamed of. For this right is not a human right that everybody is born to, but the right of the citizen to vote freely without being ordered around by anybody, the right to help run the government of his own nation.

Most of the representatives of the many, many countries in the United Nations, when Article 21 came up for discussion and voting, must have felt like leaning back in their chairs and smiling cheerfully as at an old friend, for ever so many nations, from Switzerland to the Philippines and to the South American countries led by Bolivar, had, long ago, said, "Yes, of course," to the idea. The American Declaration of Independence in 1776 had put the principle this way: "Governments derive their just powers from the consent of the governed." A hundred and seventy-odd years later the United Nations used these words: *"The will of the people shall be the basis of the authority of government."* But it is the same idea which for centuries has been spreading from one country to another.

The United Nations added some details which have been learned by long experience about how to make the great idea work in practice. One of these details that you might not think of, without a lot of experience in elections, is that people are more sure to vote as they really wish, if nobody else knows which way their votes are cast. And it is important that elections should be held often enough so the votes really make a difference in what the government does.

These working details are fairly new. But the idea itself that governments are made for men and women, and not the other way around, is an old, old friend to the human race. In many countries, the news of the adoption of this Article by the brand-new United Nations stirred echoes of national joybells ringing out long ago for a free nation, and heartfelt thanksgiving that, the older this idea gets, the better and finer and truer we all see it to be.

ARTICLE 22

Everyone, as a member of society, has the right to social security and is entitled to realization, through national effort and international cooperation, and in accordance with the organization and resources of each State, of the economic, social and cultural rights indispensable for his dignity and the free development of his personality.

Here we arrive at a turn in the road! Step by step, till now, the Articles in this Declaration have kept pushing ahead in the same direction. In history, too—which is of course just the story of our human family—there is a straight stretch of road, lasting so long that it has become familiar. And then a turn in a direction quite new and different.

For generations, men and women who love freedom and want to share it with others have been building and opening up, mile by mile, a main highway which might be called the road to political

freedom. This too was once new and unknown and unexplored. Hundreds of years ago, ordinary people were not considered to be citizens with the rights and freedoms and responsibilities of political equality. All kinds of fences kept most plain men and women from setting foot on that great highway of citizenship. Liberty-lovers have fought hard, in more and more countries, to break down these barriers and let into their full political rights a larger and larger number of human beings.

This fight to share political rights with everybody was a long, tough, dangerous, heroic struggle. There were plenty of setbacks as well as gains. People often thought there was no use going on trying. Just as soon as more freedom was won in their country, there would be a swingback, and somehow a bunch of bosses, or tyrants, or gangsters —or maybe just one boss, or one head gangster— would be giving orders to the rest of the country, and getting a hundred times more than their fair share of everything.

Yet somehow, in many nations, the fighters for freedom have won more often than they lost. There really is ever so much more political freedom for the people of ever so many countries than in earlier centuries. There was great rejoicing when, of late, it began to seem that the road was almost completed, that soon every grownup would be free to vote at elections, and that these elections—not kings, or emperors, or dictators—would decide things. Those who had been laboring with all their might to construct the road to political freedom drew breath, and lifting their heads from their work, looked forward to see how close they were to the end of that great highway.

What they saw startled them. As they had thought, they were close to completing the road of which they had hoped so much. But now they saw that the human journey leads on beyond the road they had built, makes a turn, takes another direction. They were astonished to see that there are human needs which are not met by political and legal rights—by the citizen's free vote, equality of all before the law, the right to protection of the law, and all the rest of what we have so far been reading about in this Declaration. These needs must be met by other human rights—

the right to be free from the terrible fear of not having enough to eat; the right, when somebody in the family is sick, to call in a doctor; the right for all children to have equal opportunities — really equal—for health, and hope, and the kind of education each one needs to develop the best in him.

A lot has been done, as is shown by the new schools, new hospitals, new nursing and public health work, the supply of plenty of clean water to everybody without his needing to pay for it when he gets it, the new help given to people out of work. Yet even in the freest, most modern countries, with plenty of money, there are still people in desperate need of this sort of help. Even now there isn't enough of it to go around. We must keep on working hard to make more people free of disease, ignorance, fear.

And in poorer countries, in nations where these modern ideas of human needs haven't been much talked about—there is so much still to be done! There are so many sick children and grownups

without any doctors or nurses or hospitals or medicine, or even food, to help them get well. There are so few schools, and so many people who haven't been taught that they can be helped by modern science to be healthier and more skillful, to produce more food and better food, to be more vital and hence happier.

All this was something that hadn't been thought of by those many splendid workers for human liberty who had laid out and opened the road to the freedom to vote. Many of them were taken aback and even alarmed when they saw that to enable every grownup to be a free citizen is only part of securing a fair chance to every human being to become the best man or woman possible. They saw that for that next stretch of the human journey, the road is not even surveyed and planned—let alone built. They had worked so hard to build the road to the freedom to vote that they knew a thing or two about how hard it is to lay out and open a new road. Many of the older people felt tired at the very idea.

But luckily there are always younger people growing up, just as the older ones begin to get tired and discouraged. Their eyes light up when they see this Article 22, standing at the turn of the road, like a great signpost with a notice on it, reading, "Now, we must have some Articles in this Declaration which recognize the kinds of human rights and freedoms to which men and women are entitled, not because they are citizens in some special country and can vote, but just because they are members of the human family. Unless everybody in the human home is healthy and well developed and strong and hopeful, the rest of the family won't get on nearly as well as it might. To open up the road for this new stretch of the human journey will be the hardest kind of work. There are ever so many ways to go wrong, to get lost in the wilderness. To find the right direction to take, and get the way laid out and built—that will be as long and as hard a job as it has been to open the road to political freedom.

But when did human beings ever lie down and give up their roadmaking because it was hard?

ARTICLE 23

(1) Everyone has the right to work, to free choice of employment, to just and favorable conditions of work and to protection against unemployment.

(2) Everyone, without any discrimination, has the right to equal pay for equal work.

(3) Everyone who works has the right to just and favorable remuneration insuring for himself and his family an existence worthy of human dignity, and supplemented, if necessary, by other means of social protection.

(4) Everyone has the right to form and to join trade unions for the protection of his interests.

Article 23 points out the various rights and freedoms which people have, not as voting citizens, but as useful workers. It is by working that everything fine and valuable gets done. It is by working that men and women gain their livelihood. So it is important that in their work human beings should have special rights and freedoms and living conditions, special rights equally with other workers which allow them to do their work just as skillfully, energetically, and well as is possible for each one of them. There should be equal pay for equal work—and it should not matter whether you happen to be a man or a woman. You should have some protection against the time when you are out of work. And if you want to join with others of your fellow workers to discuss conditions of work and pay with your boss you should be free to do so.

All this is in Article 23. And of all the points raised, one of the most important is the right to choose one's job. This is something basic, something that goes right back to our most elemental requirements and desires.

Babies love to play with a rattle. Just to shake it up and down pleases them. Yet as they grow, they always lose their taste for rattles. Did you ever know a six-year-old who had any interest in such baby play? From that age on to twelve, a boy or girl wants to play tag, or jackstones, or blindman's buff, to jump rope or throw a ball around, or play with dolls. They can't imagine how they ever could have seen any fun in sitting still and shaking a rattle up and down.

But they keep on growing, and by the time they are in their teens, they feel that same way about spinning tops, or playing cops and robbers or "London Bridge is falling down." That's all right for their little brothers and sisters, but now, they can't see any more fun in tag or dolls than in shaking a rattle. Now they want to be part of a team playing some kind of ball game against another team of their age. They love to run races, or to see who can jump the highest or dive into deep water most skillfully. Or they run miles in playing hare and hounds. They'd be dreadfully bored if they had to play the simple games they liked when they were five- or six- or seven-year-olds.

Well, that's the way it is with work. People keep on growing, you know, after they are through their teens. And as they grow, most men and women get so deeply interested in the work they do, and so proud of doing it well, that they can scarcely remember when they would rather play hockey or run races. It is hard for younger people to realize, but it is true, that able-bodied grown-

ups with sound minds would be dreadfully bored if they had to play all day. Life wouldn't seem worth while to men and women without the satisfactions they get out of working.

That is, if they are suited to the work they do; if they think it is worth doing; if they feel they can learn to do it well.

For there are all kinds of work, just as there are all kinds of human beings. Some folks love working outdoors and going through adventurous ups and downs. There are people who are happiest when taking ships across the oceans, through storms, or going on long journeys into deserts looking for minerals to mine, or digging up ancient ruins to see how people lived thousands of years ago. Others don't like active, irregular, risky adventuring. If they were forced to do that kind of work, they wouldn't do it well. They'd rather learn about medicine and biology so that they can be doctors or do research in laboratories, or spend hours looking through microscopes. Or maybe they'd succeed best in manufacturing, or in painting pictures, or in commerce, or in teaching, or in composing music, or in building houses.

Of all the rights and freedoms in this Declaration, there is not one which is more important to human happiness and contentment than the right to work, and to choose freely whichever kind of work each person likes and can do best.

There just aren't words in any language strong enough to express the importance for men and women of getting into the right kind of work. Anybody who lives in idleness has the worst kind of bad luck, no matter how much money he has, compared to anybody who has found work he likes and can do well.

There are so many different kinds of work needing to be done in the world, that everybody should easily find the sort which best suits his tastes and

abilities. *But only if he is allowed a free choice.*
And there are so many ways to prevent young
people from choosing freely, that we are all needed
to help keep that road open.

One of the barriers to choosing freely is just an
idea in people's minds that some kinds of useful
and needed work are inferior to other kinds. This
barrier is one of the very worst, because, since you
can't see it with your eyes, only with your brains
and good sense, you often don't realize it is there.
Take the son of a factory worker: he hasn't a
chance to choose his life work *freely,* if all the
people around him think that factory workers' children should work in factories like their parents.
Suppose the son wants to be a scientist, or an artist?

It's even worse in the other direction, when, for
instance, the barrier in people's minds shuts off the
son of a scientist or an artist from being a carpenter
and building houses. If that is what he really
would like to be, and if he can't choose that kind
of work without having everybody say it is a pity,
because the son of a scientist ought to be a learned
man—he's not "free to choose."

Since this barrier is made up of thoughts inside
people's heads, we can all help push it down by
taking care that we think straight about the *free
choice of work* as one of the greatest good fortunes
young people can have.

ARTICLE 24

Everyone has the right to rest and leisure, including reasonable limitation of working hours and periodic holidays with pay.

THERE'S A LOT OF WORK THAT MUST BE DONE everywhere. No matter where or how men, women and children live, somehow they must get enough to eat, have some clothes to wear, have a roof over their heads; the things they use must be kept clean enough so that they don't make people sick; roads must be made and repaired so that people can get from one place to another; children must be taught what they need to know to keep life going straight when they grow up; sick people and very old folks must be taken care of; quarrels must be settled as fairly as possible—well, there just isn't any end to the list of work to be done.

There's so much that if it isn't divided up fairly, some people will have more than their share to do, so much more that they never get a chance to rest and have some fun. One of the things all young people will have to see to, when their turn comes to manage life, is to try to divide up the work so that everybody gets his share of rest from work and everybody does his share of it.

This is the fair thing of course. Anybody can see that it is morally right.

But there's another very important, practical, common-sense reason for everybody's having a chance to rest once in a while. It is this: everybody can do his job better if he can count on a regular let-up. What we all need is to have the necessary tasks done. Well, they are better done if nobody has to keep at work all the time.

It took a long time, hundreds of years, before human beings could believe that. They thought that if a man or woman got a certain amount done in an hour, why, the more hours he worked, the more work would get done. In arithmetic, that's the way things go. The more figures you add to a column, the bigger the sum total. But you can't run human doings by rules of arithmetic, any more than you can tell what the weather is going to be, by adding and subtracting. If too many work hours are put into anybody's day, he doesn't accomplish more, but less. He gets so tired and discouraged that he doesn't get as much done in those long, long hours as somebody does in shorter hours who comes to labor fresh and strong.

Not only is it morally the right way to manage human life, to divide up work and rest so that nobody has too much of either—it is actually the best way to accomplish things. Just as a matter of plain fact, more and better work is done when those who do it have regular chances to rest and to do something else that they enjoy.

That's the way we human beings are made.

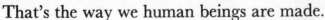

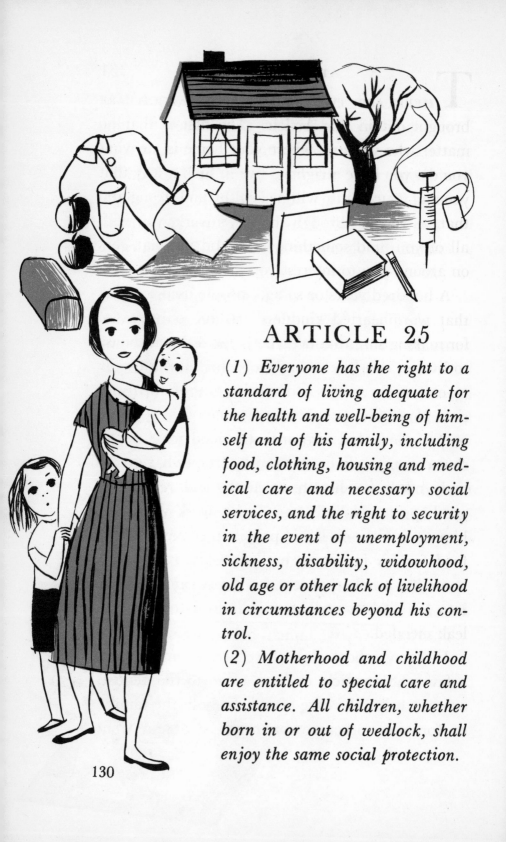

ARTICLE 25

(1) Everyone has the right to a standard of living adequate for the health and well-being of himself and of his family, including food, clothing, housing and medical care and necessary social services, and the right to security in the event of unemployment, sickness, disability, widowhood, old age or other lack of livelihood in circumstances beyond his control.

(2) Motherhood and childhood are entitled to special care and assistance. All children, whether born in or out of wedlock, shall enjoy the same social protection.

130

THERE ARE TWO MAIN POINTS WHICH ARE brought out in this Article. The first is that no matter who you are, where your home is, or what you do, you have a right to live in such a way that you and your family will be healthy and strong and that, as you go through the day's work, you will, all of you, find something in it and in what goes on around you to interest you and to enjoy.

A hundred years or so ago, people used to think that warmhearted kindness was the only reason for making sure that everybody has a decent house to live in, can buy enough food for all the family to eat, and can get a doctor if any of them are sick. Nowadays people have learned that it is not only kindness but also ordinary good sense not to shut out *any*body or *any* family from what everybody needs for health, strength, and reasonable good spirits. Nobody can do his work well if he himself is sick, or if his pay isn't enough to buy food for his family to eat, or if the roof of his house has a hole that lets down a stream of water into his kitchen and he can't afford to have the leak mended.

In every school class there are, on most days, a few who are sick, or have to go to the dentist, or must help take care of somebody in the family, or for some other reason must be absent from school. Just so, there are among people who earn their livings some who for a while can't be on the job. Sometimes a man is sick, himself, and must take time off to get well. Sometimes he doesn't get well, but goes on being sick. Sometimes there are people who are old and weak and can't go on working at all.

A man who has had a bad fall and broken his leg can't go on working in the fields or woods, or repairing automobiles, or building houses, as he does when he is in good condition. A mother with a number of young children, whose husband has been killed in an accident, can't for some years go out to earn the living for the family, because her new baby and its little brothers and sisters have to have somebody in the house with them to take care of them till they are all old enough to go to school or work for themselves.

Or maybe—this happens too, sometimes—a worker is perfectly well and strong and able to work but his job has gone, because of some change or bad luck. In the United States, before electric refrigerators were invented, there were many jobs for men in factories which manufactured iceboxes, and for men who cut ice on ice ponds in the winter and in summer carried the ice around every day to housekeepers in their kitchens. When people began to use electric devices to keep their food cold, all those factories closed. All the workers in them lost their jobs, and so did the men who cut ice in winter and carried it around to people's houses in chunks in summertime. Other workers might lose their jobs because somewhere in the world it is a bad season for farming. Maybe there wasn't enough rain and the plants in the fields dried up and died, or maybe there was too much rain and floods came and spoiled the crops. When there are no crops to be harvested, there is nothing for thousands of field workers to do.

Are there any rights and freedoms for men and women who don't work because they can't? The minute anybody even asks that question, he knows the answer is "Yes."

If it is not their fault that they can't work, if their being idle is because of something they can't prevent, they shouldn't starve, or not have a doctor when somebody in the family gets sick, or have to dress in rags which make them feel ashamed and hang their heads when other people look at them.

People haven't had time to learn as much about the new part of the human road to rights and freedoms as they have come to know about political freedoms. For a while, all they could see was that it wasn't right or decent or kind to let people starve or get sick, even if they couldn't work. But little by little, as we explore this new stretch of the road humanity is building, we begin to see something else, now so plain that we can't understand why it took so long to get it through our heads. This is the idea, now plain to many people, which was so new:—it is not only wrong and unkind to let part of our human family live so poorly that they get weaker and have poorer health than others—it is plain, ordinary common sense to give them a help

over a hard place in their lives, because in so doing, we are helping ourselves.

Take sickness, for instance:—if the family of a workman who is sick or who can't find a job, have too little to eat for too long, some one of them, maybe several, are apt to get tuberculosis. This is not only sad for them but dangerous for us all, because tuberculosis germs do not stay put in a poor home. They go right out of the door, to drift up and down the street where we and our children come and go. Or maybe one of the children needs some dentistry done on his teeth. Rotting teeth aren't catching like tuberculosis and other diseases. But they threaten the welfare of others, just the same. For the child with bad teeth is poisoned by their decaying in his mouth, he doesn't grow up strong and well with energy to do good work, but listless and weak, so that when his time comes as an adult to do his share of the needed work of the world, he hasn't the strength or the interest in living which normal people have, and so can't do his full share.

There is such a lot of work to be done, that if he doesn't do his share, those who are strong and energetic have to do more than their share, and help him, all the years of his weak life, just because nobody helped his strong father over a few years when he couldn't work, although he wanted to.

ARTICLE 26

(1) Everyone has the right to education. Education shall be free, at least in the elementary and fundamental stages. Elementary education shall be compulsory. Technical and professional education shall be made generally available and higher education shall be equally accessible to all on the basis of merit.
(2) Education shall be directed to the full development of the human personality and to the strengthening of respect for human rights and fundamental freedoms. It shall promote understanding, tolerance and friendship among all nations, racial or religious groups, and shall further the activities of the United Nations for the maintenance of peace.
(3) Parents have a prior right to choose the kind of education that shall be given to their children.

IN MODERN TIMES, TO KEEP ANYBODY FROM
having an education is rather like tying a bandage
over his eyes and making him try to find his way,
blind, among people who can see. A blind man
doesn't have half a chance compared to people
with good eyes. A person with no education doesn't
have half a chance compared with those who have.
Hundreds and thousands of years ago, this was not
so true. In the woods, in a jungle, in a little village
where he has always lived, a man doesn't need to
know how to read. If there's no path in the woods
he guesses where to go by the sun, or the stars, or
the way the streams run.

But a big modern railway station is full of
printed signs telling a traveler which door will
take him to the trains, which to the street, which to
the ticket offices, which to a place where he can
get something to eat. He is lost if he can't read

them. When he buys a ticket, he can't be sure, except by reading it, whether it's the ticket he wants. And he can't depend on other people to tell him. Maybe somebody would tell him wrong. He'd never know.

In more and more places modern life is like that. You don't know which way to go if you can't read.

Children who are sent to school and learn to read and write and figure, don't always realize that the chance to learn those lessons is their chance to learn how to find their way around after they grow up. The more they learn, the more they will be able to understand what's going on around them when they are men and women. If they don't understand, they'll be like helpless dogs or cats or horses, pushed and shoved into a railway train or truck, led along to be sold—they won't have any idea where they are going or whether that's the place they'd like to be.

As to studying and learning more than only to

know how to read and write and figure, that's just as important. Modern life has grown to depend more and more on everybody's being educated. In the old days, anybody with good sense could lay out a footpath to connect one village with another. It could be steep, narrow, muddy, stony—and still serve well enough. But to lay out a road straight enough, smooth enough, well enough made for big trucks to carry heavy loads over—that takes planning by people who understand modern engineering. Even the men who take care of such a road need to have more learning than their great-great-great-grandfathers had to make a little rough footpath to walk over.

Now it takes years of studying to understand engineering, as well as very good brains. Any student, anywhere, no matter what his race or color, who has the head for learning, should have the chance to study such advanced subjects as modern medicine, engineering, music, mathematics, art, navigation, mechanics, philosophy, architecture. Human society owes him this chance not because it will be a good thing for him personally, but because it is better for everybody. Each human group should have its full share of learned people of their own kind to teach the young, to practice medicine, to understand business, to create works of art, to manufacture machinery and use it well, to write fine books, to lay out waterworks, to study astronomy, and to construct big buildings.

It's now been found out by careful scientific research that all races have about the same proportion of people having superior character and with good brains. Not to open the doors to advanced modern education to all such specially superior individuals is as foolish as it would be to use axes made of extra-fine steel for digging in the ground. Axes misused for digging would be poor and dull-edged as axes, and they wouldn't be much good for digging either.

People who live on rich soil and don't use it to grow food are wasting something that is needed by all humanity. It's just as much a waste not to provide for every young person the kind of education which suits him best.

ARTICLE 27

(1) Everyone has the right freely to participate in the cultural life of the community, to enjoy the arts and to share in scientific advancement and its benefits.

(2) Everyone has the right to the protection of the moral and material interests resulting from any scientific, literary or artistic production of which he is the author.

ARTICLE 3 REMINDS US ALL THAT EVERYONE has the right to be alive and free, and the duty to let others be alive and free. That lays a foundation.

Now, a foundation isn't good for much unless something is built on it. Everybody knows that the way human beings build what they need is by work. The idea in Article 23 is that men and women must be free to work, and must let others be free to work, because there is so much to be done, and

141

because doing work that is worth while is the greatest satisfaction human beings can have.

But there's one chance for misunderstanding. The word "work" is often taken to mean making or growing something needed for our bodies to use—roads, schools, farms, factories, clothes, gardens, shops, shoes, houses, bridges, ships—and all the rest. Our bodies need such things.

But our bodies too are only a foundation which needs other things built on it—things like learning, the arts, the life of the spirit. Scientific study and learning, like building bridges, can be done only by hard work. Yet if you look at a man like Einstein, one of the greatest scientists alive, all that you can *see* is that he is a frail old man making black marks on sheets of paper. Compared to a broad-shouldered, mighty-muscled workman, high up on a tall building bang-whanging away at steel beams, a silent mathematician leaning over his table doesn't seem to be working. But the success of a great deal of material effort depends on his doing his work well. For the medical researcher, the astronomer, the laboratory scientist, the agricultural expert, the mathematician, are all trying to cast more light on the way the material world is put together, and every new ray of light from their laboratories helps the workers who are building and making and growing things.

There is the poet, too. He certainly does not seem to be working as a farmer works, getting in the hay before a rain comes. But once in a while, from the work of a poet, a painter, a writer, an inventor, something shines out which by its beauty or insight or a sudden glimpse of a great truth, also casts light on our human existence, what it means and why it is worth living. Our everyday life would be shadowed and dull, tiresome and discouraged, without the beams of light which are thrown from those who work hard in the arts and the sciences, trying to find out more about the place of human beings in the universe.

Of all human beings who labor, such creative workers need freedom most. A scientist in a laboratory trying to discover exactly what happens when a piece of wood is burned, must be free to discover what he really does discover. It is a dreadful waste and destruction of the most valuable human qualities if—this, alas has happened in our human past!—he is told, "No, we don't want you to discover that! That doesn't fit our plans. You must pretend that what you find out from your experiments is the opposite of what you really do find out." That doesn't hurt him like beating him with a club. It hurts him much more. It hurts all of us. It steals from our future the best possibilities we have.

So when you read over this Article 27, take a deep breath when you come to the word *"freely,"* and sing it out loud and clear, for that's the real point of this Article—everybody's right *freely* to share in free creative thinking, which is the most important kind of work that humanity does.

Of course there is another kind of "freely" which means financially free. We have the right to the free use of libraries, art galleries, and scientific museums. Especially in the case of libraries the word "freely" is important. For not only do we all need freedom to use the books in public libraries, but the books on those shelves must be freely *chosen* to preserve the best of what men and women have discovered and thought and felt, in our time and long before our time.

There is much we don't yet understand about human life and how best to live it. We need every ray of light we can get from the minds and hearts of those human beings who are living today, and from the record left behind by those who lived before them—the record of what they found as they searched for what is true, and what is right, and what is lovely.

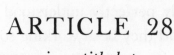

ARTICLE 28

Everyone is entitled to a social and international order in which the rights and freedoms set forth in this Declaration can be fully realized.

SOMETHING HAPPENED IN THE DISCUSSION about this Article different from that about any other Article. Quite a few of the members of the committee thought it would be just as well to leave it out.

This was not in the least because they objected to the idea in it. Nobody did. All it says is that everybody's country should try to invent ways to put into practice the splendid ideas about human life contained in this Declaration. None of the people who had voted "Yes" to Article after Article, would dream of voting "No" to the idea that the nations of the world ought to do their best to base their governments on these ideas.

But if they agreed with the Article, why in the world did some people on the committee seriously think the Declaration would be just as good without it? It was because they thought that Article 28 was only saying over again something that was already perfectly understood by everybody. Why else had they been working so hard to find out just what they could all agree on as the right way to arrange human life, if not in the hope that the nations of the world would try to arrange the life of their people according to those ideas? Why have a separate Article saying that we all ought to try to make it possible for everybody to have these rights?

This sounded so much like common sense that even those who wanted this Article left in could not at first think of arguments on their side.

Then as they talked it over, these men and women who had been for two years giving their lives to the Declaration remembered that common sense is not everything. Into their minds came the realization that there are sides of human existence so great, so lofty, so creative that they can't be put into ordinary factual, "sensible" words.

They had been laboring with all their might, for a long time, on something tremendously needed by their fellow human beings. Their hearts were full of the deep feeling with which they had been working for us all. As they looked back, at the end, on the statement of human rights which they had built up, they were moved to say something which would remind everyone that they had not

made it up out of their own heads, but had created
it out of what is in all human hearts.

One delegate found a way to say what they
all wordlessly felt, and suggested that "it seemed
appropriate to state that human beings have *faith
and hope* in the possibility" of making human life
better by putting into practice, in everyday existence, the best of what they all really know to be
true about the way to manage human life.

"Faith and Hope"

It is in the beautiful light from these two noble
words that this Article should be read.

ARTICLE 29

(1) Everyone has duties to the community in which alone the free and full development of his personality is possible.

(2) In the exercise of his rights and freedoms, everyone shall be subject only to such limitations as are determined by law solely for the purpose of securing due recognition and respect for the rights and freedoms of others and of meeting the just requirements of morality, public order and the general welfare in a democratic society.

(3) These rights and freedoms may in no case be exercised contrary to the purposes and principles of the United Nations.

Here is an Article which, although it is a long one, in three parts, is easy for anybody to understand. Anyone, that is, except a baby or a quite little boy or girl. A baby expects, of course, to get what he needs and wants without doing anything for anybody else. But it would be a really young child who wouldn't see the point if you told him, "Look, it is all right for you to bounce your ball outside where you don't bother anybody. But it is not fair for you to throw it around in the room where Mother is trying to get our dinner for us."

Long before he is old enough to read a book or to understand such words as "limitations determined by law solely for the purpose of securing due recognition and respect for the rights of others . . . ," he knows well enough what the *meaning* of that phrase is—that he has a right to play as he likes, but only so long as he doesn't keep other children from playing as they like. He often hates to give up having his own way, he often forgets. We all do sometimes forget to do what we know we should. But he learns while he is still very young that if he is going to live with others, he hasn't any right not to let those around him have a fair share of what they all want.

He may be so little that he doesn't know the *word* "duty," but he understands the *idea* all right. And as he grows, his brain grows, he comes to see that "having duties to the community" means doing just what he has always known he should do— his fair share of what everybody in the family has to do to have a home they like to live in.

ARTICLE 30

Nothing in this Declaration may be interpreted as implying for any State, group or person any right to engage in any activity or to perform any act aimed at the destruction of any of the rights and freedoms set forth herein.

EACH ONE OF THE OTHER 29 ARTICLES HAS reminded us of something we all have a right to do or to be. They all say, "Yes," and open a door. Here at the very end is one which says, "No," and slams a door shut.

You'll understand this if you will put yourself in the place of the Third Committee which worked so long and thought so seriously about this Declaration. If you were trying to do something like the same piece of work, you too would end a list of rights by a firm statement of "no right at all."

The intention of the Third Committee isn't so strange or unknown to us as to make it hard to imagine ourselves in their places. We might, almost any group of us, find ourselves asked to serve on a committee to plan for the use by a lot of different people of different ages of a playground, a library, a repair shop.

We would make a list of the ways in which people were free to use these different places. For the library, we would make an Article saying that everybody is free to use the books and papers who will make as little noise as possible (since people who are reading and studying need to keep their minds on their books).

Freedom on the playground doesn't depend at all on having silence. Just the opposite. Much of the fun in playing is in making a lot of noise. So here your statement of rights wouldn't have a word in it about not talking loudly. In a part of the playground where there were some trees, maybe some rocks, perhaps a little pond, as well as some open ground, you would put up a sign something like the following:

All boys and girls are free to use this area for games like playing tag, and blindman's buff, and jackstones, and spinning tops, and playing "London Bridge is falling down," and fox and geese, and leapfrog, and sailing toy boats.

In another part of the grounds, broad and smooth and level, your sign might be:

Free for ball players. Any member of any ball team — hockey, soccer, and the like—is free to use this field.

An open corner of the field with no trees, but with some ups and downs in the grassy surface, you might mark:

Free for kite flyers.

In the repair shop, with its shining, expensive, well-kept tools, it would be easy for your committee to agree on a sign reading:

Free for the use of serious, responsible, trained mechanics.

When you had put up a carefully considered sign in all these places, the members of your committee might say, "There! That covers everything, doesn't it?"

But no list can put in every single detail that might be thought of. It would be as long as a big dictionary if it did. One of your committee might say after careful thought, "But see here, suppose a person with bad intentions, looking for some way he could avoid doing the right thing, invented a way to interfere with these freedoms, some way which never occurred to us?"

Yes, the rest of your committee would see that danger, once it was mentioned. In the library, for instance, you had tried to protect the freedom of readers to be quiet. But suppose somebody wishing to interfere with that freedom began—*silently* —to pull the books away from those using them, or to mix up the cards in the catalog. If anybody objected, he could say, "I'm not making any noise."

What would your committee do?

You'd write at the bottom of your list something like this:—

"What we all want is to make life, as we lead it together in the library, playground, and repair shop, peaceable and orderly and useful, with an equally fair chance for everybody. If somebody does something *not mentioned by name* in this statement, interfering with other people's right to freedom in the proper use of what we have in common here, we want to say *now* that he has no right to do it. The general idea on which we are all agreed is perfectly plain from these statements about our common freedoms. Any action which opposes that general idea is wrong."

What Of It?

WELL, THERE IT IS.

And what is it now we have it? It is building material for the only bridge which will let us keep on along the human road, the road which our forefathers have been laying out, section by section, and then building, section by section, ever since there were any human beings.

That road has led us now to the brink of a dreadful, black chasm, so deep that if we fall into it that fall will be the end of us. The name of the chasm is war—total world war. If we can get a bridge made across that, we can go on building our human road into the future.

That bridge *can* be made! We know what material is needed for it—understanding among all the people on the globe and a general agreement that all humanity is so much alike that what happens to any of us makes a difference to all of us.

Do we really have as much general agreement as that to construct the bridge with? Yes, we have. That is what the United Nations Committee has been doing—gathering together and putting into one list the human rights we agree on. There are more of them than we realized we had. There is plenty of agreement. This Universal Declaration of Human Rights is strong enough to make the bridge across the chasm which keeps us from world peace. There they are, the heap of things we agree on, piled up where we can see how big a pile they make.

But a heap of even the best material isn't a bridge—isn't anything. Not yet. It must be turned into what we so desperately need. The delegates to the United Nations, the members of the Committee which has collected the parts of this Declaration, can't do the building. There aren't nearly enough of them. They have shown us that we have what it takes. But all of us will be needed to put it into shape so that we can use it to get across the great chasm—the danger of war—into world peace, which is the only place we can all go on living.

Young people are especially important for this great construction—partly because they are stronger and have more years ahead of them for work than older people, partly because their ideas usually aren't so set in old ways as older people's. When they see something which must be done, they are apt to roll up their sleeves and go right at it, because they are fresh and still have all their strength, unused. They have so much vitality they enjoy using it, as older people used to when they were young.

There's the picture—the human road leading right up to the edge of destruction. On that edge, all ready to be used, the heaped-up human agreement about what is the right thing to do as shown in the Universal Declaration. The plan is laid out, ready to use those materials to build the bridge to peace. The crowds of people are there who could do the work.

Let's go. It would be too foolish if we didn't.

Index